THE
CONSUMERIST
MANIFESTO HANDBOOK

> NO CONSUMER OR ANIMAL WAS HARMED
> IN THE PRODUCTION OF THIS BOOK.

STERLING
New York

An Imprint of Sterling Publishing
387 Park Avenue South
New York, NY 10016

© 2011 by Charles Selden
Illustrations © 2011 by Allison Meierding
Cover and book design by Allison Meierding

ISBN 978-1-4027-8648-8 (hardcover)
ISBN 978-1-4027-8943-4 (ebook)

Library of Congress Cataloging-in-Publication Data

Selden, Charles J.
  The consumerist manifesto handbook / Charles J. Selden.
    p. cm.
  1. Consumer protection. 2. Consumers--Psychology. 3. Customer relations. I. Title.
HC79.C63S44 2011
381.3'4--dc23

2011027779

Distributed in Canada by Sterling Publishing
c/o Canadian Manda Group, 165 Dufferin Street
Toronto, Ontario, Canada M6K 3H6
Distributed in the United Kingdom by GMC Distribution Services
Castle Place, 166 High Street, Lewes, East Sussex, England BN7 1XU
Distributed in Australia by Capricorn Link (Australia) Pty. Ltd.
P.O. Box 704, Windsor, NSW 2756, Australia

For information about custom editions, special sales, and premium and
corporate purchases, please contact Sterling Special Sales at 800-805-5489
or specialsales@sterlingpublishing.com.

Manufactured in the United States of America

2 4 6 8 10 9 7 5 3 1

www.sterlingpublishing.com

THE
CONSUMERIST
MANIFESTO HANDBOOK

THE GUERILLA'S GUIDE TO MAKING

CORPORATIONS PAY FOR FAULTY GOODS,

SUBSTANDARD SERVICES, AND BROKEN PROMISES

CHARLES J. SELDEN

STERLING
New York

Once again, for Patricia

CONTENTS

THANK YOU, WE VALUE
YOUR PATRONAGE

CONSUMERIST MANIFESTO
AND PLEDGE OF ADHERENCE

When, in the pursuit of customer satisfaction, it becomes necessary to dissemble and deceive corporations, my regard for the opinions of my fellow citizens requires me to explain why.

I hold these truths to be self-evident: Consumers have certain unalienable rights. Among them are truth in advertising, perfection in products and services, and a limit of three minutes to reach a fully knowledgeable person in Customer Service.

But when a long train of abuses by corporations reduces consumers to desperation, it is our right—it is our duty—to throw off such oppression and create new ways of gaining consumer satisfaction. The tyranny of corporations is pervasive and growing:

- *They deceive and manipulate consumers.*
- *They rush to market before products and services are ready.*
- *They know but don't tell consumers about defects upon delivery.*
- *They systematically reduce product quality but not price.*
- *They turn customer service into a maze of dead ends.*
- *They waste consumers' time through all of the above, and in other ways besides.*

Therefore, I solemnly pledge that I will treat offending corporations as they treat consumers. I shall pursue them on the Internet. I shall battle them on their own toll-free lines. I shall expose them to my friends. I will use the one weapon against which they have no defense: laughter.

And I'll get them to pay for my trouble.

THE WAY THINGS ARE
(AND WHY I LIKE IT THIS WAY)

According to Mario Puzo, author of *The Godfather*, great fortunes start with a crime. In my case, it was a laundry detergent. Years ago on the way to the Laundromat, I bought a box of Lever Brothers' VIM. It was a new soap that claimed, "VIM will get your clothes 20% whiter." All Lever Brothers' retail products promised that if the customer was not completely satisfied, the purchase price would be refunded.

After I washed my clothes, I wrote the company:

> *VIM is the best laundry detergent I have ever used. As great as it is, it only got my clothes 17.4% whiter. I am not completely satisfied. I want a refund because you promised 20%.*

Someone at Lever Brothers mailed me a 1-pound box of VIM—hand-wrapped and leaking soap granules, but sent in good faith just the same. It was followed by a refund check with a letter:

> *Dear Mr. Selden: We are sorry VIM did not meet your expectations. Under separate cover we have sent another box. Enclosed are a refund check and coupons for more VIM. We hope you'll try VIM again. By the way, Mr. Selden, has it ever occurred to you that your clothes are dirtier than most?*

I liked Lever Brothers' style. When a tube of their usually reliable Stripes Toothpaste ran out of red stripes before the white stripes, I wrote them again: "I paid for stripes but did not get them. The red were gone before the white." A different customer service person wrote to ask if I still had the tube for company engineers to study. I tried to help: "The red stripes were heavy at first but petered out halfway through the tube. Sorry, I do not save used toothpaste tubes." Just the same, Lever Brothers sent a refund check for the flawed tube and coupons for more tubes.

For the record, these encounters with Lever Brothers were in 1964. Their gross value was $24, based on the worth of two checks, a free box of VIM, coupons, and enough toothpaste to brush after every meal for months. These days, $24 may seem like chump change—until adjusted for the 605% rate of inflation since 1964. A $1 purchase in 1964 would require about $6 in 2011. In terms of buying power, $24 is roughly $145 in 2011 dollars.

NEARLY 50 YEARS OF VALUE

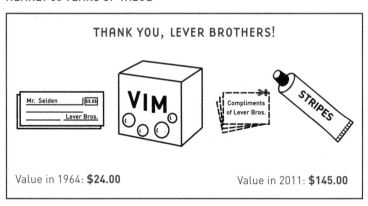

THANK YOU, LEVER BROTHERS!

Mr. Selden | $5.55 — Lever Bros.

VIM

Compliments of Lever Bros.

STRIPES

Value in 1964: **$24.00**　　　Value in 2011: **$145.00**

My Lever Brothers complaints grossed more than what I paid for the original purchases, which is only fair, considering the time and effort I put into the exchange. Looking back, Lever Brothers launched my career as a consumerist. I want to publicly thank them: Without their inspirational letters, checks, coupons, tubes of toothpaste, and box of soap, I would not be where I am today: Over $100,000 richer in corporate compensation from cash, credits, and free products. My teeth are really clean. My clothes, well, they're clean enough.

Nearly five decades later, I am in even hotter pursuit of the crimes committed against us consumers. We are being underserved more than ever. Especially when we buy the basics. We want clothes, appliances, health care, apps, tickets, computers, ice bags, underwear, and food that do their job at a fair price. We want to get what we paid for. And when we don't get it, we have to fight for it—and if we don't fight, then we are accepting less than what we deserve.

* * *

Corporate *abuse* of consumers is as traditional as fireworks on the Fourth of July. That's right, I said *abuse*. Is there a better word than abuse to describe when companies pretend to be concerned about customers but then make it impossible to talk to a human being about the product or service those customers have purchased?

How many times have you heard the recorded voice reciting the line "Due to heavy call volume..." while you wait and wait on the phone for customer service? As your frustration mounts, so does the probability of your hanging up and letting the company off the hook. As your resolve weakens and you consider hanging up, remember that the call-volume increases are likely the end result of corporate greed.

For instance, most companies are comfortable offering faulty products because it increases profit margins, but because good customer service is expensive and doesn't directly contribute to the bottom line, the same companies want to minimize the number and quality of operators on hand to respond to consumer complaints about those products. That's double jeopardy for the consumer. (Those operators—when and if you can reach them—are often speaking to you from overseas. Sure, workers at foreign-outsourced centers can answer the phone and may even speak your language, but understanding the problems of callers in another country is another matter.) The final result in too many cases is that the customers will not be heard in any meaningful way. If you think of the modern corporation as the *RMS Titanic*, that "Due to heavy call volume..." line would be: "Due to not having enough lifeboats, most of you are about to drown."

"WE VALUE YOUR CALL"

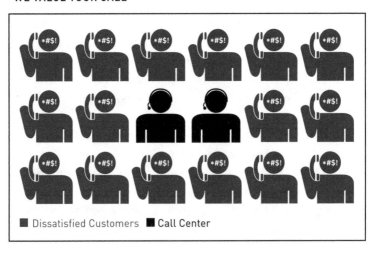

■ Dissatisfied Customers ■ Call Center

Of course, customer complaints arise toward the end of consumer-corporate interaction. In many circumstances, we are wronged way before we buy. Companies in every industry from agriculture to technology knowingly and unknowingly rush defective products to market. And throughout the industrialized world, especially in the United States where product safety regulation is woefully inadequate for the volume of product that floods the market, corporations either look the other way when their outsourced manufacturers cut corners for products once made better domestically, or they are simply unaware that corners have been cut (usually because the outsourcing takes place in a faraway country with weak safety regulations).

In 2007, the toy sold in the United States as Aqua Dots (an import from the Australian toy company Moose Enterprise) and Bindeez elsewhere was the subject of a multinational recall when it was discovered that the Chinese manufacturer that had been engaged to mass produce the award-winning toy for the international market had substituted GHB (the "date-rape drug") for one of the chemicals originally used to maintain viscosity in the toy's paint "dots." According to the then-deputy director of the Consumer Product Safety Commission, at least two American children who swallowed some of the brightly colored, gumball-sized paint beads (and one can only guess how many more worldwide) lapsed into nonresponsive comas. Why did this disaster happen? Because GHB is several times cheaper to produce than the nontoxic chemical it replaced and did the job just as well. Profit margins were increased to be sure, but at a terrible cost to the worldwide consumer.

Corporations can manipulate Internet and TV images with underhanded and undetected (ie., subliminal) tactics in advertising to sell consumers products and services they do not need, or wind up choosing for all the wrong reasons.

Will that new brand of body wash really make young men so irresistible that nearby, scantily dressed young women will soar through the air like iron filings to a magnet every time the stuff is applied? Will one tooth-whitening toothpaste really brighten your white and pearlies more than another? Do we need blindingly white teeth at all?

This is just the tip of the iceberg, of course—the list of abuses goes on and on, as we will see. But the very notion points to one fact: Though corporations like to say they love us, they sure as hell don't love as much as they say they do. If they did, they wouldn't abuse us the way they do.

THE UNSPOKEN WAR

In my estimation, industries are in a tacit coalition to wage war on consumers. No blood is shed (we presume, but it's best not to rule it out), but it *is* war, and we, the consumers, are among its casualties. The adversary's tactics are characterized by a kind of psychological warfare made possible by for-hire regulatory protection and the myth of the free market. Strategy is devised by generals in Armani suits, who gather intelligence at meetings, learn from each other's campaigns, collaboratively purchase the goodwill (and advantageous legislation) of elected government regulators through direct contributions to their campaigns (or via those goodwill ambassadors known as lobbyists), fund shoddy university research to support shaky claims about their products, and devise many other schemes besides. And all this in an effort to wring out maximum profit at consumers' expense. In a word, the field of corporate battle is rigged.

As with many wars, this one is a struggle over valuable resources—our money being the main one, of course, but certainly not the only one. As we know, corporations want to charge as much as possible for as long, and for as little in return, as possible. And in pursuit of this, they will stop at nothing. They have even seized the air! In the United States, at the time of this writing, the Federal Communication Commission (FCC) is proposing (or being pressured) to allow telecoms and cablecasters to divvy up the very air (or at least, the electromagnetic fields for which air is the medium). Arguably, this is *public property*, and something for which the media corporations that now lay claim to those bandwidths used to pay hefty licensing fees to the government to use. But now it is at auction, so that a juicy slice of the broadcasting spectrum can instead be used to carry mobile device traffic. Sure, some of the proceeds of the auction will be diverted to the U.S. Treasury, but in the long run the beneficiaries will be the new media, now locked in battle with the old media over these licenses. Consumers are left to shake their heads at all this, much the way that the Native Americans must have when the Europeans arrived with their wacky notion that owning the land, the water, and the sky was perfectly natural.

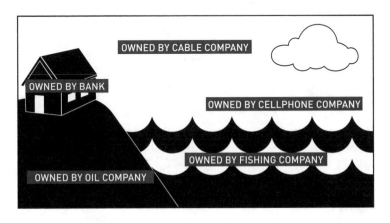

DISTRIBUTION OF WEALTH

In the marketplace, you can take money from most of the people most of the time for the benefit of a few honchos all the time. Giants of commerce have gorged on that principle since ancient times, but the concentration of wealth has been on an exponential and widely acknowledged increase of late. Indeed, this increasingly narrow distribution of gigantic amounts of wealth from corporate profits continues to outrage everyone but the elite population of fat cats who take bigger and bigger slices of the pie (in particular, the speculative banking community that exists to make money by playing with money, producing nothing of real value in the process). This is mainly because a sizeable percentage of that money is spent on purchasing governmental support for the gigantic tax loopholes, corporate protections, and the like. Since abuse of consumers expands corporate profits, a consumerist like me wants some of the extra revenue to be redistributed to consumers. But if they don't want to share, and if the elected officials are unable or unwilling to help, then it's up to the consumerist to take some of that money back.

THE NEW MARKET STATE

At this moment in history the United States is undergoing the spread of the *market state*, an ideal aimed at expanding opportunities for the individual, by which I mean the individual corporation. We used to be a *nation state*, a nation with a more collective mind-set—a nation of individual people. Then corporations had a revelation that transformed what was once regarded as their enemy into their new best friend: the government. Knowing a good investment when they run into it, corporations have figured out numerous ways to purchase the support of our elected decision makers.

Take, for instance, the 2010 Supreme Court ruling in the Citizens United v. Federal Election Commission case, which states that the sky's the limit for corporate spending on an independent political broadcast during an election campaign. How better to buy favor (or put down a threat) than with a big-budget movie that promotes (or defames) a candidate? And how better to get the kinds of laws and regulations you need to avoid pesky oversight than to have those laws delivered by government room service hired through said big-budget movie? But we don't have to rail against the system to take what's ours. Remember: A highly profitable corporation is a highly profitable target for a guerrilla consumerist.

We could fret that our turn to the market state has let outsourcing mushroom uncontrollably and wring our hands over the nation's Faustian bargain with Chinese manufacturers: They build stuff cheaply for us, but as a result we are damned by a market overrun with flawed goods. (Not to mention, a huge portion of our unsustainable national debt is now held by Chinese concerns.) *Or,* if we adopt the attitude of a consumerist guerilla, we can exploit some of the consequences of farming out manufacturing to far-flung lands. If there is now a greater chance of defects in the flood of poorly made products from overseas, that means more chances for a consumerist guerilla to collect. Just don't let the kids chew on any of those Chinese-manufactured toys.

DON'T TRY WINNING THE WAR—JUST WIN THE SKIRMISHES
Here is the key to this handbook: I am not trying to change what corporations do. I don't think I can. In fact, I have no delusions about any consumer movement winning victory

in the overall war—even if consumers wear anti-corporate, slogan-riddled T-shirts, march on the capitals of the world's industrialized nations, and regularly attend the cinematic exposés of such provocateurs as Michael Moore, Morgan Spurlock, and their like. Instead, and probably much to the horror of most consumer activists (whose work toward the greater good I applaud and support), I am content to spend my time and efforts to win the skirmishes.

Given the size, power, and swiftness of corporate growth, the practical consumerist's answer to corporate abuse is to modify classic guerrilla-warfare tactics to beat corporations at their own war games. When faced by an overwhelming force, everyone knows it is absurd to fight the enemy head-on. Find the soft spots instead—and then exploit them.

My biggest complaint is that too many consumers surrender without a fight. They accept getting ripped off as the price for how enterprise must work. The enemy wants consumers to be bound by that way of thinking. But suppose a consumer no longer accepts things as they are? Suppose the consumer demands compensation for trouble caused by corporate abuse? That's when the jungle warfare begins. Armed with your outrage and the know-how you pick up in this book, you will fight as never before. You will win much of the time. You will have fun. How sweet will that check or wad of coupons be with a few laughs to go with it?

Here are three compelling reasons to wage a consumerist guerrilla war:

Measurable compensation. The right actions get you cash, credits, replacements, points, coupons, and occasionally a melon

FedExed to you because the one you bought never ripened. A consumerist guerrilla is not easily bought off, but does not object when it happens. Compensation is to be measured objectively by what was won and how much time and money was spent to win it. For instance, $10 for a ten-minute effort is the equivalent of $60 an hour. (How much do you make per hour?) Chapter 8 shows an efficient way to calculate your rate based on measurable compensation. (Incidentally, upgrades are OK but are not counted as cash-like compensation in this handbook. Corporations go for cash, so do we.)

Comic relief. People live longer if they laugh a lot. As good as the money has been in my consumerist career, the comedy has been better. There is endless comic material when a corporation tries to convince a consumerist that the corporation is not to blame for what they both *know* the corporation did to the consumer. Like any comedy club, AT&T Wireless could have charged me a two-drink minimum when each of seven so-called "service professionals" had a different reason for why my AT&T DSL line switched on its own to dial-up from high speed. Each "reason," including that it was rival Verizon's fault, was nonsense. Nonsense is basic to comedy. Later, AT&T paid for my wasted time by issuing dollar credits on my account. I got a cash equivalent *and* the last laugh.

Genuine satisfaction. A guerrilla beats the system. Since corporations proclaim concern for high standards, guerrillas get to enforce *really* high standards for everything they purchase. I find that the standard of *perfection* works well. I want perfect products and services. When the enemy falls short of perfection, I attack!

INDUSTRY-SPONSORED ABUSES

Corporations are members of industries. Abuse by a corporation takes on new meaning when recognized as part of an industry-supported activity. For example, the cablecaster Comcast reduces subscribers' freedom of choice by requiring the purchase of a **bundle** (see glossary) of channels even if subscribers are interested in only a few of those channels. For that matter, in many markets it is almost as expensive, or in some cases more expensive, to get cable Internet without cable TV than it is to get the services bundled together. Comcast's competitors do likewise, making it a "standard industry practice."

The industry-does-it assertion is a handy subject changer to avoid answers to the consumerist questions, "Why can't subscribers have complete freedom of choice?" and "Why don't I pay proportionately less for one service on its own?" The cable industry does not want to go down that road, given the issues that might sprout like flowers after a spring rain: How did the cable industry get such pervasive control over consumer choice? Why does it seem as if the FCC is more concerned with cable industry needs than consumer well-being? When corporate abuse flows from industry power, consumers are in deep water.

LEARNING FROM THE ENEMY

Guerrilla training starts by getting inside the heads of well-trained executives and high-level managers. The language they use is a tip-off to their mind-set. Words like *strategy, tactics, head count* (a phrase for how to keep track of people, alive or dead), and *mission*—terms frequently deployed by those in the executive suite—are military expressions for planning battles. Why use words of war if you are not at war? Corporate language reveals how execs intend to *manage* and *engage* us when we are in their areas of operation, which include shopping malls, airplanes, supermarkets, department stores, and websites. They use the same terms when they infiltrate our computers to spy on us, put junk in our mailboxes (real and virtual), autodial calls to our Do Not Call–registered phone numbers, and transmit texts to our cell phones. Let's not forget when they put advertising on billboards along our roads, blimps in our skies, and prop planes over our beaches.

Corporate marketers like the sound of *target marketing* and the new technique of *personalized marketing* via the Internet. Is there a target on your back? Yes, there is, even if you cannot see it. It is drawn there in virtual invisible ink after you buy anything (unless, of course, you shop exclusively in a cash-only world). Marketers know where you live and how you live. Your spending habits are almost as particular to you as your DNA.

As guerrillas, we should admire the professionalism of corporate skullduggery, much the way the FBI admired Willie Sutton, the prolific bank robber who said he never carried a loaded weapon into a stickup. There is much to be learned from the tactical expertise of the countless corporate executives who have *never* been convicted of fraud, tax evasion, embezzlement, price-fixing, influence-peddling, or any other of the numerous infelicities that might have been laid at so many of their feet.

But their crimes need not go entirely unpunished. You're going to learn how to turn the tables on your product-pushing adversaries and make *them* the targets. Veterans of anti-corporate guerilla campaigns prefer the softest targets with the deepest pockets and the weakest defenses. More often than not, after

GUERILLA WARFARE FOR CONSUMERISTS

My mission is to empower and entertain you by exposing how corporations mistreat consumers. Perhaps you have not thought of yourself as a victim of corporate abuse. Trust me: You've been victimized. If you purchased any product or service since 232 BCE (when tribune Gaius Flaminius Nepos redistributed Roman land to the poor plebs left homeless as a result of the First Punic War), you've been manipulated, swindled, ignored, or just plain ripped off.

Your mission is to identify the specific abuses by which you've been taken to the cleaners—and how to turn them into assets that yield compensation. Luckily, consumerists have developed handy labels over the years for the purpose of identifying the specific means by which you've been taken to the cleaners. Let's look at the list:

TURNING ABUSES INTO ASSETS

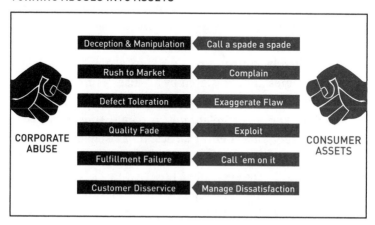

A note on the word *mission*. It is one of many business terms you'll see throughout this handbook. Mission is a favorite in graduate business schools. The institutionalized business education that provides such vocabulary, philosophy, and tactics can be adapted to serve consumerist guerillas in their pursuit of compensation from abusive corporations.

The abuses on the previous page do not always reveal themselves in their natural order. A consumer's first encounter could be with any of the six. *Customer Disservice* can reveal a *Defect Toleration* that leads to the realization that a lot of problems were already there when *Rush to Market* was put into play. *Collateral damage* from two or more abuses is a compensation opportunity made in heaven for a battle-hardened guerrilla consumerist. And sometimes a consumerist will hit the jack-pot: A chain reaction involving all six abuses. But I am getting ahead of myself.

Organization matters. This handbook's *organizing principle* (another high-impact phrase from the business school curriculum) shows the potential gains when consumers treat corporations the way corporations treat consumers. Abuses morph into assets to be exploited by consumers. This book adapts business school strategies and, bolstered by a sense of fair play and a dash of justice, arms consumers for the fight.

Part One, "Be Ever Vigilant for Corporate Abuses," is basic intelligence about the enemy's tactics. It has a chapter devoted to each of the six abuses and includes how they are handled by certain industries. The encounters I selected are like case studies, another useful tool in a business school education. It may seem like I have always triumphed, but that is not the case. Even though I have been a consumerist guerrilla for nearly four decades, I do not win every fight. And I do not always get as much compensation as I might have been entitled to. In the end, though, I can tell you this: You won't get a thing if you don't fight back.

Part Two, "Fighting Back the Right Way: Get the Cash," is advanced training. Chapter 7 dissects the enemy's mentality. Planning and fighting go better when you understand how the enemy's mind works. The chapter therefore proposes a strategy modeled on how West Point focuses cadets to move their minds "toward a personality-based understanding of the networks of super-empowered individuals that comprise the most dangerous enemies the United States confronts today."[1] This chapter helps you learn from the enemy and teaches two essential lessons: *Take as much compensation as you can get, and think about your consumerist bottom line.*

Chapter 8 provides tools and weapons for consumerists, often shortened to WMD (Weapons of Management Destruction). There are charts, forms, and other tools that will save you time, focus your efforts, and maximize your compensation in the battles to come.

Part Three, "Resources," has four appendices:

Appendix A: *The Corp-Speak Glossary* defines words and phrases, some common (and some I invented because they really should exist), that reveal how the corporate mind sizes up the consumer. It is like hearing language spoken off camera by MBAs and other Biz-Management Professionals (**BIMPs**). You need to know how they talk about you, because it reflects how they think. Many "inside business" terms appear throughout the book, and others are included in the glossary because people should know how top corporate management thinks.

Appendix B: Two forms are here. The first is designed to help you "quantify" an abuse committed against you. The idea is to help you define the value of the abuse for the purpose of describing it in ways that get the attention of corporate types whose job it is to separate consumers who mean business from those who will easily go away if ignored or discouraged. The second form is a checklist of acceptable compensation. Use this to be sure you haven't left anything on the table.

Appendix C: *Further Reading and Useful Websites* provides annotations about books, columnists, and websites concerned about consumers. There are many websites devoted to uncovering information about current or past scams. They can also get you in touch with organizations that can help sharpen your attack for getting compensation. But be cautious: It can be difficult to verify a website has verified anything on its site or that its information is still relevant.

Appendix D: *Book Club Action.* Authors are often encouraged to include notes for book clubs. Since I spent much of my career developing textbooks and teacher's guides used to wake up students and instructors, I used those methods in the book club notes. If you choose this book for your book club, I have done my best to make that session, shall we say, "lively." Let me know if it works: **c.selden@stanfordalumni.org**.

NOTES AND NOTATIONS

- A **bold word or phrase** means it is defined in the Corp-Speak Glossary.
- Notes linking to the text appear at the end of the Resource section.
- *Comp* is my shorthand for compensation.

Inflation is always with us. To illustrate the buying power and current dollar worth of my past comps from corporate abuses, I use **www.usinflationcalculator.com**. These days inflation is not much of an attention-getter—until you see its cumulative effects for more than the past two or three years. During periods of so-called manageable inflation, it runs between 2% and 3%. (Incidentally, that means a savings account earning 1% is shrinking 1% to 2% a year, and a salary raise of 4% is around 2% after adjustment for inflation.)

Your Savings Account
Not Adjusted for Inflation

Your Savings Account Earning 1%
Adjusted for Inflation

PART 1

BE EVER VIGILANT FOR CORPORATE ABUSES

There's no business like corporate business like no business I know.
Everything about it is appalling,
So much stuff regulators never see.
That all-too-familiar feeling,
When you are being treated underhandedly.

Okay, so I took a few liberties with Irving Berlin's lyrics[2], but the reality of consumers getting screwed is nothing to sing about. Abuse works best for corporations when two conditions are in place: The law allows the mistreatment, or at least makes it possible for regulators to ignore it, and the public accepts being mistreated. There's not much do be done about token regulation or lack of enforcement. But as a consumerist guerrilla, I embrace being exploited, because that opens the door to seeking compensation.

Each of the six kinds of abuse—Deception and Manipulation, Rush to Market, Defect Toleration, Quality Fade, Fulfillment Failure, and Customer Disservice—can occur on its own. And they can appear in combinations of two or more or, when the stars align, all six can swirl around a single product or service—this might seem like a disaster, but a consumerist guerilla sees a confluence of corporate blunders like this as a golden opportunity.

Vigilance is required at all stages of a product's life. Consumers often fall into the trap of thinking that if a problem occurs with a product or service, they will have to act within the specified time frame of a warranty. A consumerist sees a perpetually open window to seek compensation for a defective product or service: The window first opened because of a decision made by a corporation that knew better or should have known better.

A seasoned consumerist should always be alert to abuse, even if defects in the product or service turn up much later, after extended use. To quash consumer complaints, corporations work hard to train customers to accept the concept of a product's *useful life*, that is, how long the product will be usable. But to my mind, stated warranty periods are simply guidelines and not to be taken too literally. My idea of a useful life is the length of time I continue to use the product. There is at least one company with a similar philosophy to mine, which makes them a poor target for consumerist guerillas but pleasant to deal with for consumers. I'm referring to L.L. Bean, which has a 100% guarantee policy that states customers can return for exchange absolutely anything that has ever been purchased from them. That's the way I think of everything I buy.

Typically, corporations severely limit their warranties. For instance, Microsoft and Apple impose limits on how long they will offer even paid support for their software and hardware offerings. Before such a product is even released, executives have arbitrarily decided the length of its "useful life," which serves to shorten the companies' responsibility to the user. Tough luck for even those customers willing to pay for a bit of help to use an older product that really needs no replacement save for the relentless march of technological evolution and the inexorable demands of a growing company's bottom line.

A few more concepts to ratchet up your vigilance: Clustering is when a single abuse opens the spigot to release a surge of other abuses. A Fulfillment Failure defect can flow into a Customer Disservice matter and evolve by discovery of Quality Fade. I bought a $100 air mattress from Brookstone that was easy to inflate but impossible to deflate. Once I started

REGARDING CLASS ACTION SUITS

A product you own or once owned may have a defect or hazard you did not know about, but for which you are notified that you have a refund coming. Don't expect to always get it. To qualify is needlessly complicated—and that's intentional. The "class" the corporation has in mind excludes smaller folk because they don't have the resources or time to document their case. The corporations know it. The courts know it. Bringing attention to it might force companies to allocate settlement funds to us little people. To skirt social justice, class-action qualification involves research and documentation that would make finding the smallest needle in the largest haystack look easy.

In a class-action suit notice I received from the judge in charge of a case involving financial services firm UBS, he warned that any document marked with any yellow highlighter ink would result in instant disqualification. I wondered how he felt about mustard. I had shares of a stock in an investment fund managed for me by UBS. My shares qualified me for roughly $8.67, which is why UBS discouraged my participation in the suit. It basically said, "Not for you, little guy. It's small change." (Convince 100,000 stakeholders it's not for them and the payout goes down almost $1 million for the little guys and gets added to the payment for the big guys.) But how could I resist? In the complicated instructions for filing was the judge's stern warning that yellow highlighter would invalidate a claim. UBS battled my request to file until I threatened to contact the SEC (the U.S. Securities and Exchange Commission). Finally UBS sent the two key pages needed for my claim—highlighted with yellow highlighter. Why didn't UBS use blue highlighter? Because UBS knew about the yellow highlighter rule. The objective of class-action litigation is to conserve funds for corporations with big stakes in the outcome and to deter small stakeholders from making the pot even bigger.

the campaign to be compensated, the situation cascaded into several areas of abuse, giving me yet more chances to attack and get a $100 Brookstone gift card.

Clustering may appear as:

- A *slow grower*, such as the air mattress fiasco above.
- An *instant cluster* in which two or more abuses occur simultaneously, as when an expensive ticket for an opera does not come with sound. (See Chapter 7 for the tenor of the New York Opera's defense.)
- A *corporate combo* that traps a consumer in a pincer created by two corporate competitors that are unable or unwilling to restore a service botched by both of them. For example, I pay Comcast for cable TV. Comcast contracts with HBO to show a few series in the Comcast package. Something went wrong with the transmission of an HBO broadcast. Comcast and HBO blamed each other, sidestepping a solution to my problem (not for long, heh-heh).

Variations on a theme. All industries—profit and not-for-profit—develop a culture and a language to protect themselves from consumers. For example, the health care industry's first line of defense is denial that anything they do is wrong or could ever be wrong with a bill. The luxury clothing industry is more sympathetic because it enjoys mammoth profit margins, regulator-ignored price fixing, and a need to retain consumer loyalty—all of which makes it easier to pay for its crimes against couture lovers. The banking and credit card industries defend themselves on the grounds of **Usual and Standard Industry Practice (USIP)**, which means that established ways of screwing the customer should simply be accepted as part of life—no questions asked. The arts businesses strive to create illusions of not being in business at all. You risk being treated like a philistine if you suggest they are selling things—until you get your checkbook out and become a patron of the arts. Don't be fooled. Don't be put off. An abuse is an abuse. Keep your eye on the target and what's in it for you. Reject any corporate assertion that what you know is an abuse is actually as natural and necessary as sunrise and sunset.

AVOIDANCE OPTIONS

You can avoid getting fleeced by not shopping. That's not much of an option, unless you can time-travel to the days of hunter/ gatherers. Or you can avoid buying products from corporations you think are unscrupulous. But what choice will you have deciding between phone and cable TV providers that are **monopolies** anyway? You can't avoid shopping. Just remember that if you're a savvy consumerist, the price you pay now may become your profit later—and then some.

CHAPTER 1

DECEPTION AND MANIPULATION

What do Shell Oil, AT&T, Dole Food Company, the National Watermelon Association, and the U.S. Department of Agriculture have in common? Expertise in Deception and Manipulation of consumers. We'll call Deception and Manipulation "D&M" to be familiar, but they're not our friends. They clutter our minds to prevent us from making rational choices. They short-circuit our good sense for a quick sell. The good news is, consumerists can profit from D&M. But we're getting ahead of ourselves. Let's get to know the enemy first.

Like a con man and his shill, D&M work best when they work together. Deception alters reality to let Manipulation make consumers believe they are reaching their own decision. Instead, it's the decision intended by Deception. Deception would love you to think the new AT&T is better than the old AT&T, or that "fresh" Idaho potatoes bought in March were actually grown in late February in Idaho.

Contemporary D&M has roots in the propaganda tactics of World War II. Madison Avenue was an enormous beneficiary of wartime tools converted to peacetime advertising.

For instance, the "bandwagon" technique flourished in wartime to sway citizens to join what was promised as the winning side, because more people had joined it. A majority made victory a sure thing, the bandwagon plea went, and who doesn't want to be on the winning side? The strategy worked for both the Allies and the Axis. The actual statistics for how many people were behind each side didn't matter. Just say, "Everyone is joining our side—aren't you?" and the people will climb aboard the bandwagon. The Institute for Propaganda Analysis in 1938 declared the bandwagon as one of the top seven wartime persuasion techniques. In the hands of marketing Svengalis later on, however, the bandwagon became a warning to join the crowd in choosing a product or forever be left out. You won't lose a war, but you will lose peer acceptance, the message implied. One of the longest-standing bandwagon campaigns is McDonald's signs tallying how many "billions served." If you've never passed through the Golden Arches, makes you feel kind of left out, doesn't it?

We're loving it!

Where you want to be.

Wait!

Where you are without us.

D&M are dynamic. Successful D&M practitioners never stand still. New versions of old tactics pop up every season. That puts pressure on consumerists to keep up so they can benefit from the false claims and Machiavellian messages. But the payoff for the alert consumerist is worth it. Let the corporations deceive. We'll collect!

THE "BIG THREE" TOOLS OF D&M

Among D&M's many forms, three stand out for their effectiveness in parting us from our reason and our hard-earned money. Cognitive dissonance is the official term for how a message can be constructed to block thinking that detects Deception. Dissonance distracts us from rejecting the advertising. Long ago the advertising industry understood how the music in a commercial or the sight of a highly recognizable face could sidetrack negative thoughts about an ad's content. Certain hot-button words were also found to be particularly useful: *sale, new, free,* and *four-hour erection* are great performers. And that's not all that's grabbing your attention away from the actual product. Odd creatures that speak, fast-moving action, and 3-D billboards are constantly tested and deployed to disarm your message rejection and boost your message retention.
Repetition is simply repeating stuff in all kinds of media. As you begin to identify a company logo or message appearing on billboards, Facebook, TV commercials, and other venues—over and over again—you might become annoyed. But that's OK with the ad folks, because the product name lingers in your memory long after the annoyance disappears.
Disinformation tries to change the subject. It creates a conveniently untrue story to counterbalance an inconveniently

true story. Until 1964, the tobacco industry churned out what it called "scientific information" about the **benefits** of smoking. Then the industry realized how lethal tobacco is. The 1964 U.S. Surgeon General's Report[3] named tobacco as a prime cause of cancer. Big Tobacco countered with fabricated statistics to make its case that cigarettes were harmless. The industry increased disinformation to calm public concern (especially among those who were addicted), increased political contributions to forestall regulation, changed its **business model** to get ready for the loss of domestic revenues, and hired the best defense lawyers money could buy.

The pharmaceutical, agricultural, financial services, telecommunications, and exotic wildlife industries rely on disinformation. Sales of exotic pets—especially anacondas—to residents of Florida are a big business. Customers learn about growth projections of these critters *after* cute little baby anacondas arrive by UPS. Distributors play down inconvenient truths, such as that anacondas start small but can end up as 200 pounds of coiled mayhem. Their appetite for cats, dogs, and toddlers (seldom mentioned) is offset only by pauses of a week or two between meals. Desperate but well-meaning anaconda owners return them to nature, where the reptiles have no natural enemies and are genetically equipped to rival rabbits in reproduction. A day may come when anacondas outnumber Floridians. You'd think anaconda dealers would have to post a warning: *Keep children and pets out of reach of the anaconda. Call your zoo if your anaconda grows more than 4 feet long.*[4]

STORIES FROM THE TRENCHES
I want to share a few of my Deception and Manipulation war stories that illustrate how D&M can be turned back on a corporation.

Shell Oil's TV Sets: My Own Shell Game

It never occurred to me to buy a TV from Shell Oil until the company tried to sell me one. In the 1960s, the major oil companies owned chains of gas stations that sold their brands of oil and gas. No sandwiches, groceries, or magazines—they just pumped gasoline, washed your windshield, and checked your oil. Payment was by cash or the oil companies' affinity credit cards.

Then the industry got a bright idea. All these drivers who charge their purchases have established credit records. "We know where they live," industry marketers said as the lightbulb went on. "Let's sell them offers to buy things for when they are not driving their cars. Things like television sets!"

Shell Oil mailed a promotion to cardholders like me with an offer to purchase a black-and-white (remember, it was the 1960s) Panasonic TV set. It could be bought on the installment plan of just six monthly payments of about $20 each (plus interest) that could be added to the month's bill for gasoline. A brochure arrived with a friendly letter and an order card to mail back—plus a note informing the credit-card holder to be sure to sign the purchase agreement and check a box confirming the order. I mailed back the card, unsigned and unchecked.

Shell sent me a letter saying that no order could be processed without my signature and the box checked. The offer was repeated in another mailing. Shell's **repetition** got my attention: I sent the card again with no signature or check mark. The TV arrived a couple of weeks later.

When Shell's monthly statement came, it included a charge for the first installment for the TV. I paid for the gasoline only and attached a note:

I am paying for the gasoline. What is the other charge about?

Shell responded by saying it was for the TV I'd ordered. I wrote back to ask for a copy of my order. Shell sent a letter that said my order form was "enclosed," but it was not! That is Deception! Perhaps self-deception or Shell forgot to enclose it or maybe it was a sneaky way to get me to pay. I was offended that Shell Oil would stoop to such behavior—and I told them so in my next letter.

What's going on here? You said my alleged order form was "enclosed." It was not.

Shell answered with a note that tried to change the subject. It said sometimes a kid will, unknown to his parents, order a TV like the one it said it sent me. If I would return it, the matter would be closed. Before I could tell Shell there were no children in our household, in came another offer to sell me the Panasonic. (How many TV sets did Shell think I wanted?) I sent it in unsigned and unchecked, like the others. A letter came back saying Shell only ships when an order is signed and checked. I sent that letter back to Shell with this observation:

Here is your letter saying that unless I sign the agreement and check the box, no TV will be sent. Since you don't send TVs without those conditions being met—and cannot produce an order form from me—how could you have sent or how could I have received a TV set for which you are trying to charge me? Something is wrong with this picture. Produce a legitimate order or cancel the TV charge, or I'll stop buying your gasoline.

Shell canceled the charge. The Panasonic worked perfectly for sixteen years. This was an instance—perhaps historic—of an American consumer profitably using D&M on an oil company.

AT&T's Billboard

As a model for promotional Deception, consider AT&T's 2010–2011 billboard campaign that proclaimed, "AT&T Covers 97% of Americans."

To a consumerist, the billboard prompts questions like: What does *covers* mean? What is the difference between *covers* and *connects*? If covered, how long will coverage last? What about *spotty coverage*—does that count as *coverage*? If you are in the 3% group, is there any way out?

Taken literally, the ad said that AT&T covers all 310 million of us from sea to shining sea—except for a 3% group uncovered for reasons unexplained. I believed I was in the minority.

One such billboard was hoisted high near Giants Stadium in East Rutherford, New Jersey, on the highway that leads to the Lincoln Tunnel into New York City. The greater New York City market encompasses 18 million people, or about 6% of America. It is the major-major AT&T market. AT&T's next-largest major market is the San Francisco Bay area. In Manhattan my AT&T 3G iPhone gets shaky reception between skyscrapers and often none at all in buildings made with large steel parts.

Was the billboard sending a subtle message that AT&T cell phone customers en route to the Big Apple were headed for the 3% territory? I called AT&T Wireless to ask how I can join the 97% with working reception when I was in Manhattan. The answers I got (when I could connect to AT&T at all) varied from "Stay out of buildings made with iron" to "Walk faster when on the street until a stronger signal area is reached."

The Manipulation part is where the Deception part wants us to go. It has roots in the propaganda of combat and the cold war of the last century. Propaganda warfare (Propwar) aims to manipulate people to do or think something they otherwise might not have done or thought. AT&T's goal is to deceive us into believing their coverage is almost as large as the whole country and will therefore give us incredible service, thus manipulating us into buying their product.

The billboard played a part in the public relations quarrel between Verizon and AT&T over negative advertising. It got nasty and visual: Verizon used maps of the continental United States in its ads to disprove the 97% claim. AT&T used similar maps to prove it. AT&T's core argument was that there's population density in areas that a small map cannot show. In large, remote parts of Wyoming, for example, there are more sheep than people with cell phones, so, presumably, shepherds are in the 3% group. As for me—in the so-called center of civilization, New York City—I'm getting the same reception as a Wyoming shepherd. So I asked for compensation. I received a $60 credit.

WE'VE GOT YOU COVERED!*

■ Covered (97%)
■ Not Covered (3%)

*May not apply to you.

Dole Fresh Potatoes

A 5-pound bag of Dole potatoes was labeled as having "Premium Red Potatoes" that are "Fresh Pick" and had "the guarantee of our commitment to freshness and quality." I bought the potatoes in February in New Jersey. Where were they grown? When were they picked?

Dole uses similar packaging for its Idaho potatoes. I found Dole's subcontractor grower after I bought a bag in February. He said the potatoes were picked fresh—in October at harvest time. Then they were "scientifically" stored until shipped the following February to places like New Jersey.

As I always do, I saved a potato or two from those misrepresented batches and returned them for full refunds at the supermarkets. When I buy a prepackaged bag of food labeled fresh, I put any suspicious pieces—in their original containers—in the Returns Area of our pantry or in the spare refrigerator in our basement. They are ready for the next regular visit to the supermarket. Going to the minor trouble of retaining a couple of potatoes from a 5-pound bag, or even a couple of berries from a 1-pound box, nets me refunds for the entire container. Food retailers charge more for food because it is labeled "fresh," reason enough to raise consumerist **expectations**. Every potato and every berry had better be good—and fresh—or I'll expect a refund for the whole package—even if the majority was consumed. It would needlessly waste my time and supermarket staff time to calculate the value of one potato or berry. (We will return to this subject in Chapter 8.)

My family takes returns seriously, and food returns require special preparation. We hang on to sales receipts. Before we cut a so-called "fresh" papaya, for example, my rule is to remove the little sticker with the producer's name because it has the e-mail or website address for any complaint. And that's the gateway to coupons for potential replacements and supermarket refunds. We hold family meetings to review whether everyone is doing his or her part. If the Returns Shelf *and* the spare refrigerator are bare, I ask if we have been vigilant. I want an honest answer. (As consumerist guerrillas, we must constantly assess our troops' level of commitment to the cause.) We discuss whether our projected gross and net results are on track: In the course of a week of eating, has a product in any way disappointed us?

Recently, we raised our annual food refunds goal to $650, an inflation-adjusted sum inspired by the amount of the federal stimulus checks sent out in 2009. I am happy to report that in each of the last three years we have exceeded our goals. We have had the enthusiastic support of supermarket personnel who greet me with a smile and say, "Hi, Mr. Selden. What do you have for us today?"

The USDA Defends Seeds in Seedless Watermelons

You think my produce fixation is over the top? You might change your mind as to who's the crazy one when you read this. When it comes to Deception and Manipulation, nobody slings manure like the giants of agribusiness. The National Watermelon Association relies on the U.S. Department of Agriculture (USDA) to confirm that a seedless watermelon is seedless so long as it does not have more than ten seeds. That's a little like saying a gun is unloaded as long as it has only one or two bullets in it. This is what the watermelon folks wrote to me:

"Seedless watermelons" are watermelons which have 10 or less mature seeds . . . Changes to the definition for "seedless watermelons" would require an official request of an interested party to the USDA's Fresh Products Branch Standardization and Training Section.[5]

The letter's writer did not mention that the seedless watermelon sector of the watermelon industry asked for hearings to raise the number of allowable seeds to sixteen.

SMITH & WESSON "SEEDLESS"

Don't worry, it's bulletless!*

FEWER BULLETS THAN EVER BEFORE!

*One or less bullets in the gun.

A year later, I asked the USDA what I should tell my grandson the word *seedless* means on seedless watermelons with seeds. (Sometimes they exceed the legal limit of ten, which may be why hearings were needed.) Since the kid is only four, I did not think he would understand an earlier letter from David Shipman, the President Obama–appointed acting administrator of the Agricultural Marketing Service. I am not sure I understand it.

The definition is supported by today's current agronomic science, though as progress in science is made, changes in the future may include more sophisticated agronomic practices that ensure "seedless" watermelons are completely seedless.[6]

In other words, if I follow Mr. Shipman's logic, since *seedless* may someday happen, it is OK to say it has happened. I tell the kid, "I want you to learn to read labels. Just don't believe anything they say."

But, as a consumerist, my intent is not to rush the transition to truly seedless. I want to slow it down. If I could have learned when the hearings to allow more seeds were going to be held, I would have lobbied for a larger number of allowable seeds, like twenty-seven. Seedless watermelons are a terrific investment. They have a higher rate of return on equity for me than blue chip stocks and savings accounts. The math: I pay about $4 for a seedless melon. Usually they are tasty and sweet—and contain enough seeds to warrant an e-mail complaint to the producer, plus a return of a slice or seed to the supermarket for a refund and usually a free watermelon replacement. The producer then sends a coupon for free melons and often a check for the one I bought. So there you are: A $4 purchase for a melon I liked with a return on investment of $8 to $12 in melons and cash in under ten days. That's my kind of seed money.

The USDA says its mission is to encourage the growth of the agricultural industry, not to police the ads aimed at consumers. I promised you comedy, right? One producer's website actually says, "Our seedless watermelons have seeds."[7] Another explains that watermelons produce seeds "if they think they are dieing [sic],"[8] so they produce seeds to safeguard the future of the species.

None of them have taken my recommendations for more truth in labeling:

Hopefully Seedless
Somewhat Seedless
Seedless with Edible Seeds
Started Seedless but Sensed Danger

Or my other suggestion, which is based on the idea that watermelons can "think" they are dying. Change the business model by selling "worrying" watermelons as pets. Start with an introductory price of $9.99 and exploit the watermelon accessories aftermarket with little carts to pull them in and earmuffs for them to wear on cold days.

Deceptive Words Matter

The USDA can cut its budget by not buying dictionaries. It has no use for them. Take *fresh* and *local*—once again those two words are the source of fun and profit when I'm buying produce. A Kings Supermarket executive summed it up for me: *Fresh* and *local* are just "marketing words." Whole Foods, a corporation that knows how to play the green game, will not officially tell me what such words mean. The company ignores my letters, yet its stores pay refunds for my word-related complaints. A Whole Foods store in West Orange, New Jersey, advertised tomatoes—in March—from Maine, at least three hundred miles away. The sign said *fresh* and *local*, a multiple hot-button Deception. Theoretically they could have been fresh-picked in a hothouse in Maine after 15 inches of snow fell. But *local*? How far does a food source have to travel to lose local in favor of, say, *nearby* or *not too far away*?

If the agricultural-industrial complex ignores the standard dictionary definitions of words like *fresh* and *local* on fruits and vegetables in the produce section, why trust the industry to tell us anything inconvenient about the food we eat from any department in the store?

One of the most deceptive words is *organic*. Label a food *organic* (or, even better, *USDA/Organic*[9]) and consumers—especially those who can afford the inflated prices of organic foods—respond positively. They think organic food is better for them and better for the planet. If only we knew what *organic* meant. There is no standard definition. Most of the fifty states impose different criteria. When the produce is grown outside the United States, the definitions are completely up for grabs. Enforcement of any standards domestically or abroad is problematic at best. It's complicated and costly. Any claim of *certified* is as reliable and verifiable as the financial ratings of bonds leading up to the near-collapse of our economy in 2008.

THE NEW DEFINITION OF LOCAL

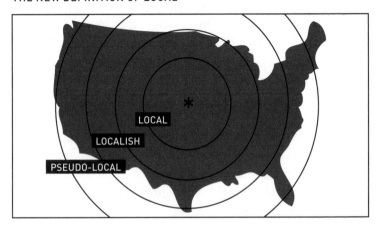

Sweet Certification and Cheating on Tests

Food inspection has become the work of a certification industry paid by the producers to rubber-stamp "organic" certification without a lot of fuss and perhaps much truth. In 2010, some foreign locations where foods to be exported to the USA were grown became too dangerous for American certifiers to visit. Certification visits were suspended in Israel, Egypt, and Mexico because of armed unrest in the growing areas. But the products kept on coming with labels claiming the goods were certified "organic" as if that meant something.

Organic certification has more variables than the number of seeds in a seedless watermelon: Certification does not necessarily cover soil treatment. Allowable growing substances are not named. We don't know who did the certification, who paid for it, how much it cost, when the produce was certified, or the size of the random samples. We don't know where to find the names of producers that applied for and any that failed a certification test. Worst of all, organic certification can be a once-a-year proposition and announced in advance to give growers time to get ready. Nothing deceives and manipulates like being able to plan ahead for Deception and Manipulation.

Claiming that food has undergone testing is another promise that often goes unfulfilled. The Brix Test, for instance, measures the sugar level in melons. A high level indicates a higher degree of ripeness. The same Kings Supermarket executive I quoted earlier candidly admitted that foreign growers might say they administered the Brix Test but he doubted they did. He added a $10 gift card to my reimbursement for my weekly return visits to the Kings produce aisle.

THE CAPTIVE AGENCY DEVELOPMENT

Powerful industries make it a priority to keep government agencies in their pockets. The term **captive agency** is understood by insiders to mean that, in practical terms, an agency listens more attentively to lobbyists from large industries because those lobbyists can influence agency budgets. They are also not above out-and-out bribery. To sweeten the pot, full-time jobs and high-paying consultant gigs often await cooperative agents. In these agencies, consumer interests are trumped by corporate interests, because consumers are not organized and have short memories while corporations are organized and know who their friends are.

The Minerals Management Service (known now as the Bureau of Ocean Energy Management, Regulation and Enforcement) is a prime example of the captive agency phenomenon. On September 8, 2008, reports were delivered to Congress exposing the MMS's acceptance of bribes in the form of sex, gifts, and drugs from energy companies in exchange for lax regulations and laxer enforcement. We all know how well that turned out for the Gulf of Mexico.

HOTELS GUESTS GO GREEN

The *green* label is moving up fast on *organic* in its looseness of definition, a boon in profitability for those industries wanting to get on board the green movement. The hospitality industry has embraced the idea of going green with a card on a pillow that urges you to *go green* by using the same linens and towels to help save water and power. Therefore, to help the planet, a guest must leave the preprinted note on the pillow to ensure that the bed will be made with the previous night's sheets. Fresh towels will be provided only when used towels are left on the floor. In other words, we are all in this together.

I wrote to corporate managers at the Marriott, Hyatt, and Hilton chains to suggest that guests be given economic incentives to keep their linen and towels longer. My idea was that guests who agree to waive linen changes share in the economic benefits by daily fee reductions of, say, $5 to $10 a day. Two responded by thanking me for my valuable feedback and promised that the idea would be forwarded to "management" (Hyatt) and the "R&D Team" (Marriott). Hilton did not answer—perhaps to save paper.

The green would fade fast if the hotel chains had to share their savings from reduction in labor, laundry detergent, water, and electricity, as well as their gains from longer-wearing sheets and towels. Conservation is important to hotels, but money is not the sort of green they're willing to share.

CLUSTER POTENTIAL

Deception and Manipulation are just the start. D&M can be a gateway to all kinds of compensation for your troubles. The guerrilla consumerist, or one in training, always investigates beyond D&M to unmask a profit-spewing **abuse cluster**. Think of it as eating a cherry and discovering an entire sundae beneath it. In Appendix B, you will find a chart that includes detection and evaluation of clusters.

ABUSE SUNDAE

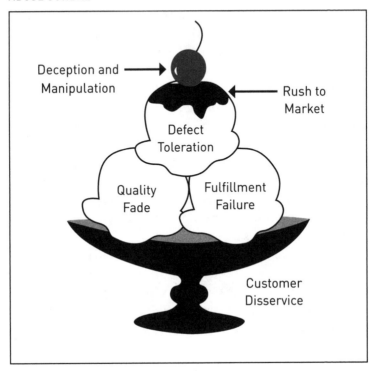

CHAPTER 2

TOO BIG TO SUCCEED MEETS THE RUSH TO MARKET

The bigger companies are, the more complicated and convoluted they become. Corporate departments proliferate; far-flung suppliers flourish without regulation; the distance lengthens between top management and consumers. Propelled by the lure to rush products to market to meet marketing promises, abuses flow like sap from an overactive maple tree.

Technology and Globalization (T&G) have accelerated the expectation of how quickly products should reach the market and get into the hands of consumers. Ten years ago consumers accepted two to four weeks as normal delivery time for ordering stuff on the phone or by computer or catalog. Now marketing tempts consumers with next-day delivery—or even same-day delivery. But there is one catch: If there are several **critical steps** from manufacturing something to actually delivering it, decreasing time between steps may diminish a few of them, like **quality control** or training service people to troubleshoot new products.

The existing systems may not be able to handle increases in speed and volume demanded by a rush to market urge. It is like installing high-speed rail cars on low-speed tracks to meet demand for faster transportation. Derailment becomes just a matter of time.

THE *TOO BIG TO SUCCEED* PHENOMENON

When a corporation reaches gargantuan levels, it becomes not so much too big to fail as it does too big to succeed. Size matters. The history of the management of large organizations reads more along the lines of rise-and-fall than rise-and-rise. These behemoths are prone to eventual failure because their very success leads to their fatal excesses: too many departments, complicated chains of command unsuited to fast-moving need for decisions, $3000 wastebaskets for CEOs, **golden parachutes** for leaden executives. The Greeks anticipated it with the idea of hubris, and we have advanced the phenomenon by allowing the likes of JPMorgan Chase, Comcast, AIG, and Fannie Mae/ Freddie Mac to grow so large that they become too big to succeed—and then they take us down with them.

Banking As a Sometimes Thing at Citibank

Citi's specialty is **hidden fees** and charges that are reversible only by the intervention of live service reps, in the rare moments they can be reached. Like other banks, Citi concocts charges and hides them to generate high profits without additional labor costs. Citi will cancel the **fees** under the right kind of pressure, but even if only a small percentage of the fees gets through, Citi makes out like a bandit. It uses its behemoth size and labyrinth of departments to frustrate customers into submission, tiring them out just with the thought of fighting through the red tape.

To complicate matters, Citibank invents services and changes procedures but does not inform the right people at Citibank about them, a telltale symptom of the Too Big to Succeed syndrome. My favorite of Citi's touted perks is linkage. Linkage is supposed to connect a checking account with a savings account as a safety net for a check that would otherwise bounce. This finicky feature is far from failsafe, as it often disappears right when you need it.

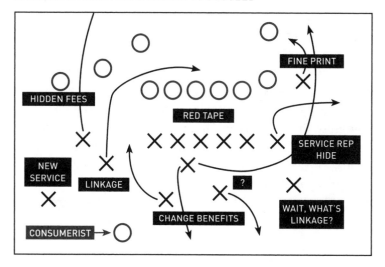

One encounter quickly put me into combat mode. My blank checks listed a New York City address for Citibank, where I mailed my deposits. Without notice to me, the operation department handling deposits was moved to the sixth floor of a Citibank building sixteen blocks away. At tax filing time, I FedExed a deposit to the old address. The deposit, a large one to cover federal and state income tax payments, was received and signed for by the new Citibank occupants who then did nothing more with it because deposits were not their job. I assumed that my deposit was at Citibank, as verified by FedEx.

I learned of the non-deposit when Citi sent a notice that my tax payment check had bounced. Where was the deposit? I had a receipt for delivery of the check to the sixth floor *at Citibank*. And what happened to my "linkage"?

Citibank's first line of defense was to blame the victim. To the corporate goons, I had sent my deposit to the wrong place. To them, it was my responsibility to keep up with the comings and goings of Citi offices. It was my responsibility to know that the address on the deposit slips was no longer valid. And, so they figured, it was my responsibility to know that the promise to link to my savings account in an emergency was not really a promise Citi would keep. To my way of thinking, the deposit went to a Citi location—and the correct one, according to my deposit slips and my past deposit history—and linkage was a policy that would serve me when I needed it.

Citi battled me, but before long the bank surrendered. If I paid tax penalties for a late tax payment because Citi did not deposit my check or alert me to a change in branch location, I would have sued for damages and expenses. I'd probably have done well with a jury whose members paid taxes or banked with Citi. Maybe Citi knew this. No doubt, Citi executives recognized that they had a pain-in-the-butt customer on their hands. Citi messengered the check to its new office sixteen blocks away after I threatened to go to New York City, fetch the check, bring it to the right office, deposit it again, and charge the bank for my time and expenses.

This squeaky wheel got greased plenty: Citi agreed to cover any federal tax penalties or late charges. (Fortunately the IRS simply redeposited the bounced check.) Citi compensated me for my time and trouble with a permanent upgrade to Citigold checking without the standard requirement of a substantial monthly balance. Ever since then—eighteen years ago—Citi has not charged me any monthly checking fees no matter how low the average balance goes in my checking account. But now and then Citi has tried to pull a fast one: A service charge once popped up. One phone call eliminated it. Years later another check bounced due to linkage failure with my savings account: Citi canceled the $30 fee and agreed to write a note to the recipient with an explanation that I was not the problem; Citi was.

A consumerist's policy with his/her bank should be this: If the bank wants to keep the account, it must cancel any hidden fees or charges that are justly complained about. Banks like Citi quickly agree because, as I said, as long as the percentage of consumers who fight fees is small compared to those who accept fees, why lose the account?

A SHORT HISTORY OF SLAMMING

The 1984 court-ordered breakup of AT&T into four entities led to an eruption of competitors—familiar and unfamiliar—raiding one another for customers. Enter **slamming**. Rogue phone companies, intent on gaining new business, dialed targets selected by area code or **data mining**. The most promising call recipients were children, teenagers, the elderly, and non-English-speaking adults. The companies would then pose a vague question, such as, "Would you switch phone companies if it was easy and saved you lots of money?" The goal was any sort of affirmation, from "uh-huh" to "Would you repeat that more slowly." Any affirmation would do to immediately switch the call recipients' carrier, whether the customers really wanted it or not. AT&T lost an untold number of customers to other providers as a result of this scam. But it never filed suit against the perpetrators because AT&T accidentally slammed its own customers using outdated phone lists. It had always been bad at internal coordination, but had never paid so dearly for it.

RUSH TO MARKET

When Rush to Market drives decisions by management, problems are bound to follow—and the chances of consumer compensation multiply. Between the time a product or service is promised and the actual date it is delivered, a shadow falls on the known-unknown: A corporation develops promotional promises based on optimistic schedules. Changes can undermine those commitments. As the unknowns become known, management gets caught between the Hard Fix and the Embarrassing Delay:

Accept what is wrong and make the delivery date.

OR

Fix what is wrong and delay the delivery.

A delay in delivery date will disappoint consumers and encourage competitors to make unkind remarks about the company's reliability. A sense of corporate self-interest will inspire a company executive usually to damn the torpedoes and Rush to Market, while plans are made to manage surges in complaints.

A savvy executive can rationalize this tactic with beautiful PowerPoint graphics that illustrate increases in sales despite increases in complaints. What would the corporation rather deal with—selling 50,000 units with 5,000 complaints (10%) or selling 500,000 units with 100,000 complaints (20%)? Doubling of complaints is offset by the profits from a tenfold increase in sales. The challenge for corporations is to reduce the costs from complaints by automating and outsourcing.

GMC's Rush to Diesel

In the 1970s, General Motors exploited the oil shortage by quickly retrofitting its Oldsmobile Cutlass gas engine.[10] The goal was to promote it as a new diesel engine to exploit the gasoline shortages and long lines at the pump for regular fuel caused by the OPEC (Organization of Petroleum Exporting Countries) boycott. I fell for it. Lines for diesel fuel were short. Diesel-car engines had a reputation for long wear.

GMC warranted the car and engine for 40,000 miles—far less than the 100,000-mile warranty of foreign makers of true diesel-car engines.

The transmission failed shortly after it crossed the 40,000-mile mark. I had no choice, said the Olds dealer, so in went the car for the transmission replacement. Oldsmobile Service charged me $495.

Since I had had the car serviced according to the manual by authorized GMC dealers, I was curious as to why a durable diesel would develop this disability so soon.

I made a few calls. One dealer surmised that the transmission fluid had not been changed, adding that it was supposed to be done every 25,000 miles. Another dealer said it should be done every 20,000 miles. The driver's manual was less precise about changing the transmission fluid, suggesting that it depended on whether the car was driven in the desert or in lots of stop-and-go traffic. I asked each one why a GMC Mr. Goodwrench—as the famous ad campaign called GM mechanics at the time—never suggested a transmission fluid change. Answer: The owner has to request it.

I asked GMC HQ (using the Oldsmobile GMC hotline), What is the failure rate for this model's transmission? Answer: less than 1%. That was untrue. GMC's rush to get a diesel car to the market had resulted in an immediate bad reputation for the Olds diesel. (No GMC dealer would take it in trade.) The reviews for this model were overwhelmingly negative.

In one last try for comp, I got lucky. I filed a claim with the Better Business Bureau. Amazing and instructive results: This claim instantly generated a form letter response, saying GMC had agreed to settle a class action suit about the car's transmission for owners who submitted a documented claim. I filed and received a check from GMC for the $495 I had paid.

Thank my consumerist stars, because the aid to most of the Olds buyers was rigged. The judge who decided the details of the class action suit put the burden of discovery on owners, not the makers of the flawed engine. GMC had no obligation to tell original owners about the decision, nor did dealers. GMC lied about the rate of failure. Few collected. I was simply lucky to be one of the few. (There will be more about class action suits and the BBB in the Epilogue.)

All Those Apps

A cell phone fueled by Apple's new screen technologies spurred AT&T to Rush to Market its 3G iPhone in 2009. AT&T had a two-year exclusive arrangement with Apple. Promotional promises emphasized abundant applications. In order for all those apps to reach all those new phones, a lot of capacity had to first be in place for incoming calls and outgoing information.

However, a new **business model** was needed to float the app promise. Conventional marketing wisdom argued that capacity to perform should precede the promise to perform. Enormous capacity would have to be in place for the 3G to deliver what was promised. But what if the new products couldn't handle the load or, for that matter, the system was overwhelmed by the load? A new twenty-first-century business model solved the problem: Do not build capacity until you can confirm demand. Demand quickly crushed capacity, a great success for AT&T but not for AT&T customers. After the onslaught, depending on whom you asked, the AT&T 3G was wildly successful (according to AT&T) or problematic (according to many customers in AT&T's two most important markets—the New York City and San Francisco metro areas). AT&T solemnly made another promise to build the needed capacity over a two-year period, emphasizing the billions to be spent but not compensating the customers who were misled. By then the two-year contracts would expire and 4G and 5G could appear, making 3G obsolete.

NEW AND IMPROVED MARKETING WISDOM

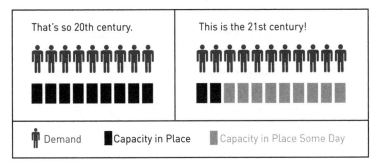

AT&T & ME: AN ODD COUPLE

I am a longtime AT&T customer/complainant. By now I imagine I am on a list that alerts Customer Service to send me to Executive Level Resolution (see Chapter 8) straight to Guantánamo Bay.

In addition to the refunds I chronicled receiving in Chapter 1 for AT&T's shaky 97% coverage claim, AT&T has credited me on other occasions. An early DSL device rushed to market, described by one of the company's techies as "a piece of crap," got me a refund after I mailed the box back to the executive offices. At a later date, AT&T tried to charge me $182 in unexplained charges for downloads to my computer that neither AT&T nor I could identify. I got the charges dropped. In addition, AT&T credited me about $120 in monthly service adjustments for the personal time I consumed dealing with untrained (if opinionated) techies. But AT&T really outdid itself when Customer Service tried to help me retrieve three messages stored on an early model cell phone.

Message Retrieval Solved

In a frenzy, AT&T pushed hard to get into the wireless market. New models of cell phones were proliferating and model changes were in the supply chain before AT&T's service people had figured out how to use the current models. AT&T's executive level saw no point investing in technical training that would be made obsolete by new models soon to replace the fleeting models being sold at the moment. This Rush to Market was accelerated by the coalescing of technological change, speed in assembly and delivery, and rising market demand. Why worry about product quality or technical support for a cell phone that was rushed to market when the next model is already in the works? And the ultimate result? I had no idea how to retrieve three messages stored in my very first cell phone and neither did AT&T.

My first cell phone came with a printed manual with nothing on "message retrieval." I tried every common sense tactic

I could think of before, as a last resort, I tried AT&T Technical Service. Techies were not supplied with manuals, and my techie was unfamiliar with my cell phone—but this lady had a shortcut for message retrieval.

She told me to punch in a code. When it did not work, she told me to punch in another code. That didn't work either. Next came the AT&T technical version of a Hail Mary pass: "Press the 8 key." I did. Messages erased.

"Hey, the messages are gone," I said.

"Yeah, that can happen. Sorry."

"Sorry? Why didn't you warn me?"

"I thought it would work."

"Now what?"

"They're gone. I can't help you."

"That's crazy. I'll cancel my contract, damn it."

"If you do that, there's a $250 early cancellation penalty. It's in your contract."

I was turned over to a supervisor who explained that the techie was new. In a service tactic that you may recognize, the supervisor tried to make the abuse acceptable by explaining why it happened. I rejected the cause-as-acceptable-excuse reasoning and stayed with the effect: Unless I was to be compensated for my loss of time and messages, I would cancel my contract and hope that AT&T would sue me for breach of contract. Maybe a judge could get AT&T to explain how RTM made AT&T omit retrieval instructions in its user's manual.

"What did you have in mind?" she asked.

"$250."

"Where did you get that number?"

"The same place AT&T got the cancellation fee."

"OK," she said. "I'll credit your account $250."

At the time, my monthly cell phone charge was about $35. The $250 covered about half a year, or 25%, of my two-year deal in 2003.

HIDING BEHIND WORDS

Any complaint line uttering the recorded "Due to heavy call volume . . ." script signals that you're probably not going to get a satisfactory answer any time soon. Once you're connected to a live person, you might also hear vague excuses, such as rumors of mergers, couched in words such as synergy, economy of scale, and derivatives of symbiosis. Corporations love to toss out baffling language to explain, for instance, why you didn't get the miracle hair restorer you ordered. And good luck to us consumers if we're trying to get answers. Outsourcing (lots more to come on this) of customer service, manufacturing, assembly, and order fulfillment to the Caribbean, China, India, and former Soviet satellites in Eastern Europe makes that nearly impossible. While you're tearing out the last teeny strands of hair on your head, the company then issues a press release denying any problems in fulfilling orders. The announcement emphasizes that consumer complaints are not unusual at this stage of a product launch, especially for a product as highly anticipated as the company's miracle hair restorer.

KIMPTON CARES

Renovation sparks RTM. Anyone who has ever dealt with a contractor knows this. The time needed to do a task expands as the promised date of completion nears. My wife and I relearned that the hard way upon our arrival at Portland, Oregon's Vintage

Hotel, recently acquired by the Kimpton Hotels chain. The Vintage's brochure quotes Mike Depatie, president and CEO: "Kimpton cares about and is committed to social responsibility."

We booked for the Fourth of July weekend in 2009. The hotel was advertised as "recently renovated." It should have said "Under Renovation." During our three-night stay, we kept reading about Kimpton promises while we waited for evidence of them to appear (like room service) or disappear (as when the rattling, roaring jacuzzi in the next room woke us up). So many promises, so little delivery. My letter to its president, Mike Depatie, summed up our stay:

The KIMPTON CARES slogan about water, air, and the planet (and presumably, paying guests) collided with reality during our three-night stay at the Kimpton Vintage in Portland (3–5 July 2009, Room 818). What should have been quiet was noisy, what should have been noisy was silent. Room Service was modeled after the old General Motors idea of defects on delivery.

We were assured [at check-in] that "818 is a quiet room." Technically, it is. But the room on the other side of 818's bathroom has a Jacuzzi that is quiet only when not in use. At 1:30 a.m. on July 4, a waterfall-like sound awoke us. It was followed by Jacuzzi activation, a roar that sounded liked a Sherman Tank had moved in next door. To honestly describe 818 as "quiet" needs the proviso "as long as no one uses the Jacuzzi next door."

The hotel has an elevator problem. It is exacerbated by consumer expectations that elevators go flawlessly up and down at the push of a button. When my wife got stuck between floors on Friday evening, she did not panic because the other guests trapped in the contraption said they had already been through this once before and eventually someone would notice—and someone did. Therefore, when I was caught in it after the doors closed around noon on Monday, my concern did not start until I realized that in addition to the DOWN and UP button failures, the ALARM button was silent. There is no phone in the elevator and my cell phone was useless in the steel cage. The OPEN DOOR button did work and, unlike my wife's adventure, the elevator was not marooned between floors but merely stuck at the 8th floor. The front desk said the engineers knew about the matter and "were working on it." The desk clerk suggested the stairs worked. (Is that the Kimpton Cares part?)

Another Kimpton challenge was Room Service delivery of a pot of coffee, hot milk, and two slices of toast with jelly—coordinated delivery, that is, for arrival of everything at the same time. On Sunday morning Room Service started with the pot of coffee, only enough hot milk for one cup, and the toast. (Are guests supposed to specify that sugar is desired, spoons needed to stir the sugar and milk, and knives needed to transfer the jelly to the toast?) A tribute to specialization followed: The harried fellow who had brought the coffee next brought the sugar. The silverware and napkins later followed, delivered by a wordless management type who looked as if, although [it was] still morning, he had had a long day. The bartender who thoughtfully added two additional cups of coffee and more toast next carried the proper amount of milk up. The episode took a while to unfold.

If they avoided the elevators, we do understand. Incidentally, the remains of the four cups, pot, creamers, and silverware were still outside our door when we returned around 11:00 p.m. So there you have it. The hotel has been open but a few months. It appears that management rushed the opening before operations were ready. . . . As for Kimpton claims about energy conservation and care about natural resources, I am puzzled by how Jacuzzis fit that profile: A Jacuzzi is the conservation equivalent of a Hummer. As for the dysfunctional alarm button in a demonstrably quirky elevator, it surely is a legal violation of Portland safety codes. (How did that elevator system get approved?) If not, guests should have been warned in advance—if Kimpton cares, that is.

At checkout Kimpton credited one night ($202.50) of the three we stayed, plus room service for the disjointed coffee service. An additional $202.50 credit arrived from Kimpton after receipt of my letter. Altogether, the credit was $441.52.

THE RUSH TO ATTAIN "NEAR-MONOPOLY" STATUS

Aside from shoddy products, another peril of the Rush to Market is that consumers get inescapably bound to industries composed of only one or two viable companies that are designed for profit but not for service. On paper, antitrust laws promote competition to protect consumers by prohibiting a corporation from becoming a monopoly, therefore fostering a marketplace where healthy competition results in better products and services. Of course, a wily executive can figure out a profitable way to work this. If a corporation cannot find any competition left standing because it knocked them all off, it just creates one because this is cheaper and smarter than running afoul of anti-trust troubles. The key word is *one*, because **near-monopolies** are better for corporations than monopolies.

In the cable industry, two will do. Any more competition than that ruins a good thing. The titans in the industry are Comcast and Time Warner Cable. Together, they successfully lobbied regulators to limit competition in exchange for the industry's investment in expansion of cable capacity in areas designated by those same regulators. The underlying reality was understood by the industry and the regulators but not by consumers: Once the capacity was in place, it acted as barriers against the entry of new cable companies. These barriers would be incredibly difficult to overcome—something like establishing a brand new public utilities company in an established metropolitan area or going inside a McDonald's and opening up a hotdog cart.

THE ILLUSION OF CHOICE: NEAR-MONOPOLIES

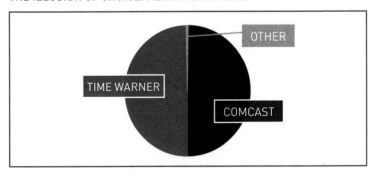

Entry to market was thus rushed in a new way: Market segments were to be handed to one or two cable companies based on a one-time vote. It is a corporate form of gerrymandering that depends on rushing a system into place with minimal competition assured by regulatory assistance. Once established, a Comcast or a Warner is free to systematically ratchet up its rates and create immutable channel packages before consumers even know what hit them. Corporations profit immensely, while consumers are rendered powerless as prices rise and extra charges are created to retain the service and pay for "special programs."

Of course, to receive cable an expensive infrastructure needed to first be put in place. However, will it ever be paid for? In exchange for near monopolies, consumers give up true choice of channels for the phony choice of bundled packages of channel: Buy a lot you'll never watch to have access to the few you want to watch—and often pay an extra premium for other programs. That part of the deal was not disclosed when cablecasters were rushing into the market, and once a large corporation reaches near-monopoly status, it holds all the cards.

NEAR-MONOPOLY ADVANTAGE

Better than being a monopoly is being a near-monopoly. It has all the advantages of a monopoly—freedom from free-market forces and guaranteed profitability—without any of the legal hazards. The hard work for near-monopolies is reaching nonviolent accommodations with competitors. Just as the Luccheses and Gambinos cooperate somewhat in industries of common interest, cablecasters such as Time Warner and Comcast are able to split up cable markets to their mutual benefit.

Pass Go, Collect $$

Comcast, despite—or perhaps due to—its near-monopoly status, is still vulnerable. Whenever there is a service disruption due to Comcast bumbling, I call its toll-free number and insist on a transfer to a U.S. office, rather than continue the conversation with its outsourced service people. The credit adjustments follow in the $30 to $40 range. Some are one-time-only credits; others are spread over several months.

For example, Comcast tried the HBO-did-it defense. HBO produces shows that Comcast broadcasts. I paid Comcast an extra fee to watch HBO Preferred Service On Demand. Comcast advertised an episode of the *The Pacific* as available a week before it actually aired. Not understanding that Comcast had prematurely trumpeted the broadcast, I could not bring up the show because it was still a week away. Comcast was wasting my time.

After being ushered into "One moment, please" mode by a Comcast techie, we figured out the problem: The availability announcement was an error. I asked Comcast—whose HQ is in Philadelphia—for compensation for the hour I lost. Comcast service tried the "blame transfer" tactic, pinning the responsibility on HBO for announcing the incorrect info. My response: "I pay Comcast, not HBO. Give me the credit and make HBO repay you. Or cancel my account." Comcast paid with a month's credit.

CHAPTER 3

DEFECT TOLERATION

The first casualty in war is truth. In consumer battles, the possibility of a corporation admitting a defect is therefore remote. In the design or production stages, defect-detection raises a central question for the company: Is it better to delay delivery to get a product right or to profit from an on-time delivery of a defective product? If management convinces itself that most after-sale complaints can be handled in ways satisfactory to the corporation's bottom line, Defect Toleration (DT) wins.

Naturally, making the decision to tolerate a defect requires a company to have customer service representatives and managers with enough chutzpah to claim **plausible deniability** with a straight face to get dissatisfied customers off the phone.

Here is an example of how the DT process might unfold when executives are confronted with a defective product:

1. What percentage of the total products is affected?
2. Are the products under our control?
3. What are our options?
4. Which fix is cheapest?
5. Is this a slow news day? If not, can we keep a lid on the story until Friday night? (Saturday media coverage is generally lighter.)
6. What do we tell customer services representatives to say to angry customers?

As we can see from the last step of the DT process, from a consumerist perspective, defects are compensation opportunities. The obstacles are what corporations erect to protect themselves from the consequences of defects. A consumerist should keep in mind that even if defects are well known within the corporation, they will be denied publicly. But the companies know what they have done. The trick for you is to make them pay.

GUIDE TO GREAT DEFECT MANAGEMENT

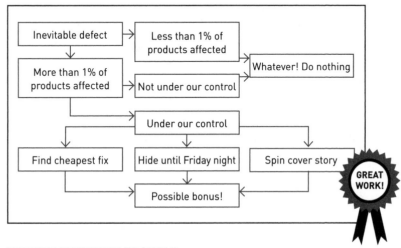

TELETUBBY TUMMY TROUBLE

In 1999, PBS ordered 100,000 adorable stuffed dolls as a promotion to lure viewers into buying a membership. Within each cuddly plush toy was a device that produced cheery talkback for toddlers. When a little kid squeezed the doll's tummy, the dolls uttered phrases like "HELLO!" and "LOVE YOU" and "HUG ME." The dolls I'm talking about were from the wildly popular *Teletubbies* series (1997–2001), seen regularly on PBS.

The Teletubbies are frolicking creatures that look part-baby, part-Martian. They did have one notable adversary, however. In 1999, the Reverend Jerry Falwell claimed that the Teletubby named Tinky Winky encouraged homosexuality in kids because of his effeminate behavior, purple color (a gay-pride color), and the triangle (a gay-pride symbol) on his head. Falwell demanded that the show be taken off the air. Let that serve as the backdrop for what happened next.

A random quality-control sample of the Teletubby named Po found that some of those dolls uttered a few lines not officially in their cheery script. Lines like "BITE MY BUTT" and "FA--OT, FA--OT, FA--OT." There were 100,000 plush Teletubbies ready to be shipped to 100,000 unsuspecting families. How did PBS manage this unexpected defect?

They shipped them.

As a consultant who helped PBS produce promotional trailers, I was privy to the behind-the-scenes goings-on in the Teletubbies fiasco. First, PBS thought my call alerting them to the problem was another one of my practical jokes. "Nice try, Charlie, but we are not biting. You've done better in the past."

"Hold on," I replied. "Listen." I squeezed my Teletubby so my PBS contact could hear it on the phone.

"Oh boy," he said. "Overnight a few."

The next day, following a top executive meeting at PBS headquarters in Arlington, Virginia, PBS made the decision to send them out—defect and all—and make sure the warehouse manager wasn't going to tell anyone else.

Luckily, there were no reported outbreaks of butt biting.

THE WILLIAMS-SONOMA HOCKEY PUCK PITCHER

I needed a new pitcher for my homemade iced tea. I went to Williams-Sonoma, the high-end cookware chain. A salesperson suggested the $20 Frigoverre, an import from Italy. I do not know how Italians make iced tea. I know how I make it: Bring water to a near boil and pour water into a 16-ounce Pyrex-type measuring cup with five tea bags, sugar, and lemon juice to taste. Brew four minutes and transfer contents to a 32-ounce glass container. Add ice to fill.

I like Williams-Sonoma. The salespeople know the products and are helpful. But neither this saleswoman nor I knew that while the Frigoverre can withstand a dishwasher and a microwave, it cannot come in contact with nearly boiling water. Recently boiled water will cause the bottom to instantly break off into a glass hockey puck, quickly followed by the contents. I discovered that the hard way on my first try. Down came the hockey puck, then a hot pond of lemon–tea–sugar water formed on the counter and cascaded to the floor.

My call to the local Williams-Sonoma store ended in the usual *Oh, my, so sorry, bring it in, full refund.* That is not acceptable to a consumerist. This is not a return; this is a *defect*. Why should I spend my time bringing in the remains of their fatally flawed Frigoverre? What is the Williams-Sonoma defects policy? Does it plan to continue to sell these fragile Frigoverres to my fellow consumers? What about the cost of the tea bags?

Williams-Sonoma is a multibillion-dollar conglomerate that owns brands such as Pottery Barn and Le Creuset. Its headquarters is in San Francisco. The trick is reaching the right department. My first call started out friendly: I wanted W-S to know of a defective product that could turn dangerous. My call was quickly transferred to claims. I was handled carefully—as if litigation were on my mind.

All I wanted was compensation. Besides, I was doing W-S a favor. It had, through no fault of its own, a mislabeled product. I had a bad experience. I was not injured, just outraged. My experience might help W-S avoid problems down the road. Claims was a dead-end destination, however, designed to deter or quickly settle with difficult consumers.

Another toll-free call led to Terri Bosworth at W-S Corporate Customer Service in San Francisco. I told her that W-S should pull the product from its shelves—and its catalogs and website—to protect consumers, and I should be compensated beyond the $19.95 to account for tax and tea bags and time.

Terri got to the point: "What do you have in mind?" I mentioned that my wife wanted a new toaster for our new kitchen. Terri said the best one was the Dualit. (It listed for $399.95 but later went on sale for $200.) It was ours if that made up for the incident. I took the deal. Minus the $20 for the Frigoverre, my consumerist comp was between $180 at the sale price or $380 at list price.

THE ROLLING RESTOCK METHOD

Sometimes Defect Toleration can sneak up on you. For years our screw-top ice pack worked perfectly. Unscrew the top, drop in the ice cubes, replace top, and apply to the area in need. When the ice melts, unscrew top and pour water out. It sells for $10, and it's made by Apothecary Products, Inc.

I bought a second one. One key difference caught my attention right away: The rubber lining of the blue original model had been replaced by a less-watertight, blue-and-white material. The original held water until the water was dumped out. The new bag was porous. Perhaps the idea was to save the consumer the trouble of unscrewing the cap to remove the water. If you waited, the water departed on its own, like a miniature glacier caught in global warming. The bag had been made in China, an outsourcing destination to be revisited in Chapter 4.

I called Apothecary Products' toll-free number in Minneapolis. An amiable manager admitted awareness of the porosity problem. That day she FedExed a replacement that was "Made in the USA."

I asked when the water-sealed ice packs would be for sale again. She told me in Corp-Speak that as the faulty ones were sold, replacements would follow in the "rolling restock" method. Translation: As soon as the bad product inventory sells out, the fixed editions are rolled in. Sell the bad stuff before sending out the good stuff. Waste not, want not.

As for my old "new" bag, CVS, the pharmacy where I purchased it, cheerfully refunded my money. When I mentioned the porosity defect to CVS, the sales clerk shrugged, "We'll report it."

THE DEVOLUTION OF QUALITY

MADE IN THE USA   MADE... ELSEWHERE

MOZART AT MIDNIGHT

Historically, the automotive industry surpassed all others in Defect Toleration. It was recently replaced by the financial services industry in 2008 in this category. It can reach the point where its defect corrections are defective. That creates multiple opportunities for compensation. I go way back with automotive

DT, but as a case study it's still useful. My second car was a 1966 Volkswagen Beetle, just when its reputation for quality was the talk of the industry.

I bought my VW from Gus Mozart Volkswagen of Palo Alto, California, then the biggest dealer in northern California. Two flaws showed up in the first month. At 55 mph, the engine, now and then, inexplicably shut off. Was this a gas-saving feature? My hunch was a loose ignition apparatus. There was also an odd vibration in the roof when the car went faster than 55 mph.

At the standard break-in service after 500 miles, I described both problems. Gus Mozart Service checked them, assuring me that the ignition was working perfectly and that the vibration was a structural matter covered by the warranty. But to deal with it, exploratory surgery would be needed. The procedure was to peel back the metal roof of the car like the top of a sardine can to see if anything was wrong with the contents. My condition was that Mozart VW guarantee no scars or discoloration in the area of the surgery for the car's life—and that it polish the car after removing the sutures. Service said no way.

Mozart went ahead with the 500-mile procedure. The engine cut out again. The vibration remained. I tried to call the service manager, but he was constantly unreachable. I asked for Gus Mozart, but the chances of reaching him at work were as good as finding the composer Mozart alive and teaching music at Stanford.

Gus Mozart lived nearby and was listed in the telephone directory. I called him at home.

At midnight.

He was not expecting my call. "Hello?" He sounded groggy.

"May I speak to Mr. Mozart?"

"I am Mozart. Who is this!?"

"I am Selden. When I try to get you at the office you are never available. I thought I might catch you at home."

"It's midnight!"

"Oh, right. Sorry. I work late and this is a good time for me."

"What the hell are you calling me about?!"

I summarized the problems and the lack of service. When I was done, he barked in an accent I've heard in World War II *stalag* films, "Bring the car in tomorrow!"

I brought the Beetle in the next morning. The service personnel were expecting me. The guy in charge of Gus Mozart Service addressed me as "Herr Selden." He told me the problems were a faulty ignition device and improper wheel alignment, both under warranty. Once fixed, it ran perfectly. Eighteen months and 20,000 miles later, a regular service visit revealed that the brushes in an electrical device needed routine replacement. When I came for the car, the service manager told me I had been designated for a special courtesy:

CONSUMERIST TIP: CALL AT YOUR CONVENIENCE

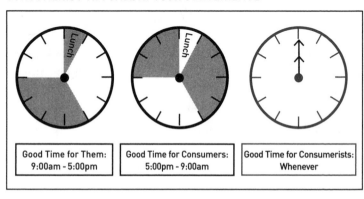

| Good Time for Them: 9:00am - 5:00pm | Good Time for Consumers: 5:00pm - 9:00am | Good Time for Consumerists: Whenever |

"This time there will be no charge for parts or labor for you."

Danke. That charge in 1967 would have been $65. Adjusted to 2010 dollars, that's $438.

CONDITION RED

While hosing the suds from my Ford Escort one day in 1990, it hit me: I was washing a *loaner*. Why should I care if it's clean? It was on loan for our Lincoln Continental, which had been confined to long-term care. The Escort was red, not a color I would have chosen. It had a small trunk. I hated it. The loaner was the most recent result of defects in a drove of repair escapades—defects several service places thought I should not only tolerate but also pay for.

The problems began when my Lincoln's red warning light went on after I inserted the key but before the engine started. To make matters worse, the warranty had expired. A local Firestone Service shop had claimed it could fix the red light by subcontracting the repairs to someone I'll call Mr. Red Light. He improved it: The red light waited for the engine to warm up, then came on. Maybe it was the extra five minutes for the red light to illuminate, but Firestone claimed there was a new problem with the light, a wiring issue that required Mr. Front End, another subcontractor. He prescribed a $960 "front-end" replacement. I charged everything on my Firestone credit card. Result: New front end done, light still went on, but at least the engine ran. This defective service would not stand.

The first bill from Firestone headquarters in Cleveland came right after the second repair. I wrote a note on the payment slip to explain that I would make no payment until after the red light problem was completely fixed and the first repair had been credited. I added that if details or verification were needed, HQ should call its Firestone outpost. I explained my policy about interest and late-payment charges: No repair, no pay.

After completion of his work, Mr. Front End was unable to explain why the red light kept coming on but assured me that the new front end was now like new.

Another Firestone bill arrived with interest charges and late fees amounting to more than $1,000. I ignored it. No fix, no payment.

Firestone Corporate turned it over to a collection agency. I proposed that we meet in court, where Firestone could tell a jury that I refused to pay $1,000+ for a twice-repaired red light that still lights up when it shouldn't.

That gets us back to how I got the loaner. I took my ailing Lincoln to Warnock Motors—then the biggest Lincoln dealer in New Jersey—and was loaned the red Escort. Mr. Service Manager diagnosed the Lincoln's problem as dysfunctional catalytic converters. Cost to repair: $2,000. He said it would take three days.

A week passed. Each time I called Warnock Service, Mr. Service Manager was "not available."

Two more weeks passed. When Mr. Service Manager remained unavailable, I insisted on a conversation with him. Enter Ms. Service Manager (no relation). She described Mr. Service Manager as "an idiot" who had recently become an ex-employee of Warnock. He apparently had promised *all customers* that their repairs would be done in three days. She confidently predicted just another week would be needed.

I periodically called Warnock for updates: I wondered about visiting hours because I missed our Lincoln and thought it

NOTES ATTACHED TO BILL PAYMENT SLIPS

Notes attached to bill payments are not read by the machines that open the envelopes. In some cases, the notes are shredded. But don't let that deter you. Write the notes. You want to create a record for the battle that lies ahead. The notes are cost-free diversionary actions. They add to the confusion corporations construct for themselves by asking consumers to mail payment stubs with payment checks enclosed. In doing so, corporations demonstrate that they are not interested in hearing from us. Just getting paid by us is communication enough. Follow-up notes that ask questions like "What's your answer to the note I sent last month?"—coupled with nonpayment of bills—put a corporation on the defensive and may cause it to trip over its inability to deal with anything other than checks. (You can accomplish the same thing with e-mails.)

missed me. On one such call, I began by asking for the Intensive Care Department. On another call I asked for a loaner upgrade into a white Lincoln. One night I fantasized about bringing the loaner in to see how much Warnock Sales would give me in trade for a brand-new Lincoln. My close friend the cautious lawyer sternly advised against this.

Six weeks after I'd brought in my Lincoln, Warnock announced that it was ready. I delayed pickup for two days. My plan was to pick up the Lincoln on the same day I was leaving on a business trip, so I could park the Lincoln at the airport in Newark, while I was gone. Warnock was outraged at the delay, threatening rental charges for the loaner and storage charges for the Lincoln.

I came for the Lincoln on a late afternoon in the middle of a sultry week in August. I paid the $2,000+ charge with a credit card. (More about the need to use credit cards in Chapter 8.) On the way to the airport I turned on the air-conditioning. The red light lit up within a minute. When I got to the airport I left a message for Warnock Service: "The goddamn red light is still on. When I get back from my trip, you will get this car, and you'd better get the repair right. And no more red Escorts."

A few days later, I returned to Newark International Airport at 8 p.m. on a flight delayed by thunderstorms. The Lincoln was right where I'd left it: in a lonely, faraway long-term parking lot where the airport bus dropped me off as its last passenger. The air was heavy with pre-storm humidity. Thunder crashed overhead. I turned the key and at that very moment rain came down in torrents. The ignition seemed to turn on the storm! Aside from that, nothing else went on—not even the red light.

I waited for a lull in the downpour. I dashed to a nearby phone booth to call AAA. (It was the pre-cell phone era.) Because of the storm, a forty-minute delay for a tow truck would be likely. I waited in my unlit, unpowered car. The tow truck arrived. However, the driver demanded cash payment for the "extra" $50 surcharge for a tow to Montclair (16 miles away). He said AAA has a 3-mile limit. I said I have expanded coverage up to 25 miles. He said nothing, started his engine, and drove off, leaving me and my dead Lincoln in the parking lot.

I spotted an Avis sign off in the distance. Between monsoons I ran to Avis and rented a car. A big car.

The next day's phone calls:

Call #1—To Warnock: Informed them where the Lincoln was and its condition. Told them to get it and not to worry about a loaner. I added that when and if Warnock gets it right, I would bring the Avis car to Warnock so Warnock could return the car to Avis and reimburse me for the rental.

Call #2—To AAA: Explained events and insisted that it delist the tow firm. AAA agreed.

Call #3—To Ford Motors, Michigan: Made a formal complaint to Consumer Affairs about Warnock's failures to repair the Lincoln.

Call #4—From Warnock: The towing service hired by Warnock accidentally punctured the hydraulic brake lines underneath the Lincoln while securing the car to the flatbed truck at the airport. Warnock promised to install a new hydraulic braking system at no cost.

The Lincoln was ready in three days. Warnock said the original work was not the cause of a "new" red light problem: By coincidence the battery had died. *Coincidence* was the word of the day: A radiator leak was a "new" problem. Warnock replaced it. When I came for the Lincoln, I asked for the old radiator. (Under New Jersey state law, an auto repair company is required to offer the defective piece to the customer.) Warnock was unable to locate it. Warnock surmised that the defective piece had been inadvertently left outside where "Someone probably took it."

Warnock agreed to cancel all charges for the new radiator and battery along with payment for and return of the Avis rental. When I declared that the $2,000 repair might have been unnecessary and the fault of the radiator, the operations and service managers took offense at any suggestion of dishonesty. Touchy people.

I wrote Ford to describe the Warnock part of this saga. Ford refunded the Warnock bill of $2,000+, a substantial sum in 1990.

THE RED LIGHT THAT STARTED IT ALL

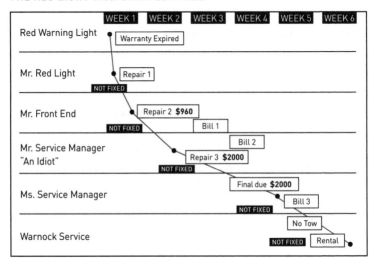

Firestone—the first to service the Lincoln—canceled all charges, including the original $960 after I sent the company the Warnock bills for work that fixed what Firestone could not.*

Warnock paid for and returned the Avis rental. About $150.*

AAA also reimbursed me for the Avis rental car. About $150.*

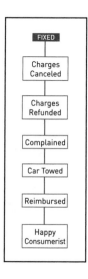

With its new front end, new radiator, new brake lines, and new catalytic converter, the revived Lincoln ran like new for another 40,000 miles. It died of natural causes, and I gave it to a charity as a tax deduction.

These amounts are based on memory, not documentation. They are close to the reimbursements I received.

CHAPTER 4

OUTSOURCING—THE ROAD TO QUALITY FADE

Quality Fade—the term, not the process—was coined by Paul Midler to describe what can happen to American corporations that outsource. In Midler's 2009 book, *Poorly Made in China*, he chronicles the growth of QF: a slow, steady and *planned* slide of product quality by Chinese companies *after* an American product line is totally under their control. Their initial offer is too good for American corporate executives to refuse: The Chinese contractors will copy every component, follow every spec, assemble, and ship—all at stunningly lower costs that compel American corporations to send manufacturing from America to China. He writes an eyewitness account from the start-up stage to the startling stage when American corporations realize that the lower prices do not stay low, even as the quality of the products diminishes. There is little that the Americans can do except go along with this decrease in quality—and pass along poorly made products to consumers.

A CAUTIONARY TALE OF SHAMPOO

In one example, Midler follows the life of an unnamed down-market shampoo once made in America in three "flavors" (for some reason the manufacturer didn't call them "scents"). Production is outsourced to a Chinese company that signs a contract promising to adhere to the original specs, but far below the original manufacturing costs. As the changeover progresses, a minor spec change by the Chinese does not set off alarms for the American company. Certification, especially on-sight inspections by outsiders coming from half a world away, becomes complicated and expensive. Cultural and language differences further confuse matters. The outsourced factory refuses to cooperate.

Finally, a cost-cutting step catches the attention of the Americans. Instead of three flavor scents, the outsourced company uses one flavor unlike any of the three promised. The Chinese, however, do not change the flavors stated on the labels, thereby not wasting labels previously printed. Every shampoo is almond scented, yet each is labeled either vanilla, cherry, or strawberry.

WASTE NOT, WANT NOT

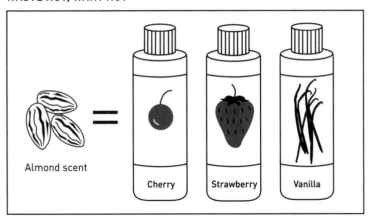

Almond scent

Cherry | Strawberry | Vanilla

From the outsourced company's perspective, shampoo "flavor" is U.S. marketing puffery because what really counts is that the product is actually shampoo, and not soup, per se. As long as the result is clean hair and a pleasant aroma, the flavor is irrelevant, no matter what the label says. Bottles not containing the same amount of shampoo is no big deal, either, especially for a shampoo that retails for a dollar. And if the shipping cartons occasionally burst because too many are piled on top of one another, or if a few bottles explode if they're handled too roughly, the low Chinese overhead eases corporate pain, the outsourced manufacturer figures. The outsourced firm, having built up capacity, then begins to eye shampoo-making competitors of its American client. Sure, the client has a contract for exclusivity. Perhaps it's enforceable in China's legal system. Perhaps not.

Complicity and Compliance

What can the American corporation do? Distributors are waiting for large shipments. Competitors might seize the advantage if delays result from the company's insistence that the Chinese meet the specs. Management knows what has to be done: Creative complicity. Make the best of a mess. The market is eagerly awaiting a cheap shampoo, whatever the flavor. The product is getting to the consumer, in spite of the bursting cartons and damaged shampoo containers. And really, what is the harm? If complaints come—"My shampoo said vanilla. This is more like almond!"—the American company whose name appears on the iffy product's label can send two coupons for 50 cents off the next bottles, along with coupons for other products. That'll shut up irate buyers. Complicity is the path of least resistance and greatest profits.

I admire what outsourced Chinese companies have pulled off. They deserve high marks for long-term planning. Quality Fade—although they would not call it that—appears to have been part of their long-term strategy from the start. American companies swallowed the bait and then recovered by doing the predictable: They passed the result on to the consumer and—if pressed—they blamed the supplier.

WARNING SIGNS OF QF

A consumerist must be alert to the signs of an emerging QF problem. Sometimes QF happens to a high-quality product or label that has been around for a while. The product has a following of loyal customers and benefits from instant recognition and consumers' long-term **satisfaction**.

QF in Pricey Powder Packaging

Consider my wife's Chanel face powder, imported from France by Bergdorf Goodman. The face powder comes in a round, black container whose lid slides snugly over the top. Remove the lid and there is a small platform that holds the puff. The platform has a bunch of tiny holes that, when the device is turned over, sprinkle the powder on the puff for application to the face. For years that platform was a separate piece that my wife could easily pry off so she could scoop some of the precious powder into a smaller purse-sized powder puff holder. I say *precious* because the powder costs $52 with the shiny box. When my wife buys a replacement, my job was to use a sharp blade to pry the platform up so she can scoop some powder out and into her compact.

Without warning, the manufacturing specs changed: The platform had been incorporated into the mold holding the powder. It wasn't apparent to me until after several unsuccessful tries with my screwdriver blade to find the ridge of the platform. The powder had been shipped from New York City to us in New Jersey. My wife's call to return it to Bergdorf's did not go well: The Cosmetics Department manager said there would be a $15 pickup charge—and we had to supply the shipper. Time to bring in the A-Team: Me.

I've been put off by every big cosmetics department I've ever visited. I sense that if the aromas will not kill me, the prices will. There are scant details about the ingredients in all the pretty tubes, boxes, and jars. Talking to the cosmetics staff on the phone isn't so great, either. In this case, I was aggrieved by the new non-lift-off platform and the idea that we had to pay 30% of the sales price to return an item Bergdorf's was going to throw out anyway. I called BG's Customer Service department and got Myra, a manager of kindred spirit. She shared my discomfort at spending more than six minutes in cosmetics and was as outraged as I was at the $15 charge to send back the powder. She canceled the charge and said keep the powder.

Was this a QF episode? Yes: I am sure the change in specs came about to lower the manufacturing cost. There are times when consumerists have to rely on experience, instincts, and presentation skills to plead their case. And it sure helps to have a customer service rep who provides service.

Beware of other QF potential in packages of established brands with words that shout to freshen a seasoned line of goods, such as:

NEW!
NEW MIX
NEW FLAVOR
GLUTEN GONE
NEW CONTAINER
BETTER THAN EVER
SAME QUALITY, NEW BOX
NOW WITHOUT TRANS FAT
NOW WITH CALCIUM ADDED
NOW IN A NEW SQUEEZABLE BOTTLE

Any of the above can also cover up that old products have undergone other less attractive changes the company prefers not to mention.

Nordstrom's Incredible Shrinking Pajamas

In 2006, I bought my first two pairs of Nordstrom's long/tall men's pajamas. They were made in China. They were everything one seeks in pajamas: They fit and did not shrink. They were actually the size indicated on the label. That's astonishing in this time when clothing size labels are more decorative than informative.

Based on that success story, I bought two more pairs in 2010, also made in China and also labeled long/tall. One pair was cotton, the other a bamboo-fabric derivative. Was it possible that in four years, all tall people—except me—had shrunk? The new pajamas were skimpier than the old ones. The sleeves from one new pair were 2 inches short of my wrists. The shirt was cut 3 inches shorter overall. The other pair's legs were 3 inches above my ankles.

I wrote to CEO Blake Nordstrom, a fourth-generation Nordstrom. I enclosed both new pairs of the too short long/talls. I knew the refund would not be a problem. However, I wanted to enforce my Consumerist Return Policy over Nordstrom's return policy. Nordstrom follows the USIP (Usual and Standard Industry Practice) of trying to collect from the unsatisfied buyer at the sending and receiving ends of a purchase involving shipment. Instructive math: A consumer can wind up paying $24 in shipping for a $75 purchase. That amounts to a 33% surcharge for the shipping and handling to receive and return a package that weighs under a pound.

Corporations make money on S&H—if you let them. They

do not reveal their actual cost of shipping. They get discounts from private shippers, such as UPS, FedEx, and the U.S. Postal Service. Handling of shipped orders is highly automated, meaning the labor charges are pretty sketchy. A $50 item can have a $10–$15 shipping charge. Its return may have a similar charge. You could wind up paying $20 for a defective item that should never have been sold, but certainly must be returned. It adds insult to injury to consumerists when a corporation pockets a profit on S&H. Or can it be that the corporation is in the S&H business?

With that in mind, I made my battle plan to confront Nordstrom. I wanted to sleep better at night, even if it wasn't in my new pajamas. My Return Policy is not to pay for S&H if I'm disappointed by a product. Period. Why pay for Defect Toleration or Quality Fade? I did not shrink the long/tall pajamas.

Nordstrom refunded all costs, including shipping, but did not implement the suggestions I made on how to align L/T size label with reality:

Size: Not As Tall As Before

Size: Not At All Tall

Size: DIY

Nordstrom HQ responded on behalf of its CEO about the shrunken pajamas:

After checking with our product development group, the rate of return for this product and from this factory is very low. This is an ongoing process, so we will keep monitoring.[11]

MUM'S THE WORD ON OUTSOURCING

A random sampling of outsourcing at three Macy's (in West Orange, New Jersey; Buffalo, New York; and Palo Alto, California) points out a contradiction in what, according to corporations, is good for consumers. In each store, women's suits came mostly from China, with some from Vietnam and Croatia. Nothing had been made in America. Yes, the prices were very low, even before generous 30–50% discounts were applied. But what is the effect on American unemployment in the clothing industry? I raised the question with Macy's headquarters. Back came this reassurance:

Our role as retailers is that of a buying agent for the consumers, and they make the final decision on the products that we offer through their buying choices.[12]

Neither Macy's nor Nordstrom would go near outsourcing. It's a third-rail word for many corporations. The standard answer is that a consumer cry for value causes corporations to outsource. As for possible emergence of Quality Fade, not to worry, things are being monitored.

SHOW ME THE GOAT

If you are shopping for a cashmere sweater, do you ask the salesperson where the cashmere came from? Do you ask to see before-and-after pictures of the actual Kashmir goat?

The best cashmere is from the chin and belly of the Kashmir goat, whose coat is harvested once a year. The only way to be certain your cashmere came from a Kashmir goat is to be there for the harvest. Or raise your own Kashmir goats. Otherwise, anything labeled *cashmere* is a candidate for QF or worse, Quality Disappearance (QD). Labeling a sweater *cashmere* is like Kraft Foods passing off *vanilla flavor* as the real deal in its JELL-O pudding. You're probably not getting cashmere, but cashmere flavoring.

If you're tempted by a $25 cashmere scarf, ponder how much of the cashmere is goat and how much is flavoring. Feel a lot of high-priced cashmere to educate your hands to the just-right soft-plush feel, although to do so might create a scene. I feel the cashmere. I do it openly. Recently I asked a manager at my Wilkes-Bashford where the cashmere in a scarf came from. Did he know whether the Kashmir goats were reproducing at record levels? He offered me a glass of water.

A quest to determine authenticity of cashmere is a lost cause. Thickness—officially the *ply* and *gauge*—is a crucial tell[13], but what clerk knows anything about that? If you are having a dull shopping day in a fancy clothing store, ask the salespeople what they can tell you about ply and gauge. Watch 'em squirm. If you buy in spite of having read this paragraph, keep your receipt. If your cashmere starts to wear or fade a few years later, send it back with a note saying good cashmere should last as long as an expensive umbrella.

HUFFERY AND PUFFERY

Support of Huffery and Puffery can become an ally of consumerists. Huffery and Puffery is a judicial precedent, not a firm law. It allows excessive exuberance in corporate promotional claims about products and services. Corporations, if pushed into court, fall back on the huff and puff defense. If it is good enough for corporations, it is good enough for consumerists. In developing a complaint about abuse, huff and puff as needed. If they exaggerate, I exaggerate. Their promotions inspire creative interpretations of what I think their promotions promised. I am exploiting the exploiters. It seems like fair play.

LIFETIME UMBRELLAS FROM PAUL STUART

In the 1980s I bought two collapsible Knirps umbrellas with lifetime guarantees from Paul Stuart, the New York City/ Chicago clothier. Both worked perfectly until a windy day in the twenty-first century shredded the black nylon, leaving it hanging pathetically on the wooden handle. Knirps no longer supplied umbrellas to American retailers but that was merely a detail: I bought mine from Paul Stuart, which promptly sent me a much better one in exchange. The other umbrella, now nearing its thirtieth birthday, is still serviceable. I can wait. The serious consumerist takes a lifetime guarantee at face value. *Lifetime* means lifetime. Even in an era of Quality Fade.

WALMART'S CERTIFIABLE

Walmart sells, for about $16, a Chinese-made two-piece digital thermometer to show temperatures of food cooking in an oven. The metal probe attaches to a plastic-coated wire that plugs into a monitor box powered by two AAA batteries. The monitor can be programmed to ring at a preset temperature. So far, so good.

I used this contraption for the first time on Christmas Eve. Customer service and corporate offices were unavailable to explain two items in the instructions, written in China:

> *5. DO NOT place display unit or wire on hot surface . . .*
> and
> *NSF certified*

How does one keep a wire from coming in contact with a hot surface when the wire goes from the pork loin inside the oven to the monitor outside? Even leaving the oven door open would not keep the thin wire safe from contact with a hot surface. And what is the NSF? Did it certify these instructions?

Unable to find answers on Christmas Eve, I used American ingenuity to keep track of the roast. The trick was to avoid melting the wire or placing the monitor in the oven and risking further problems, like spontaneous combustion of the AAA batteries. So I periodically opened the oven with one hand and stuck the probe into the roast with the same hand. With the other hand I suspended the wire leading back to the monitor.

I read the display, removed the probe, and closed the oven.
I repeated the procedure every ten minutes. It almost worked.
The desired meat temperature was 160°F. When it reached
145°F, it was nearly there. But ten minutes later it hit 170°F.
The pork roast had reached a temperature beyond the recommended perfection point. We ate it but it was a bit drier than
it would have been at 160. In other words, it was not perfect.

NSF is the National Science Foundation. For a fee, NSF
certifies things for manufacturers. I reached Mark Sanford,
an NSFer, who explained that NSF's certification of safety is
limited in this case to only the metal from which the probe
is made, nothing else—especially the instructions. I suppose
NSF and Walmart thought I should have known what was
certified and what was not certified. Walmart, intentionally
or not, was implying that NSF certification of one part of the
device certified the whole thing.

Walmart's corporate principles include "Striving for
excellence" and "Service to the customer." I wrote to Mike Duke,
CEO, to complain that the Walmart store was willing to refund
the $16 if I brought the device in, but the store ignored the
essence of my grievance. Nothing on or in the package said
what I had since learned: The wire could withstand temperatures
up to 450°F. I would keep the device, but the real point was
that Walmart spoiled my pork loin. I wanted the $22 for the
pork loin as compensation.

Duke's office sent my letter to Tim Dexter, buyer of housewares.
He sent me a two-page defense of Walmart's thermometer and
a promise that

> . . . the technical quality control group of the company who
> supplies us the thermometer . . . have committed to revise

the packaging [sic] instructions immediately.[14]

What about the $22? I wrote him a reminder that my roast would have been better had the instructions passed Walmart's "excellence" test.

A handwritten note on lined, three-hole notebook paper arrived in a hand-stamped plain envelope from Tim. The note closed with, "Here's your money," and $25 in cash.

I thought my new friend Tim at Walmart had taken the trouble to do "the right thing" until a Wade Farms refund of $20 for unripe melons arrived in the same format as the Walmart refund. Refunds have become a new way to deceive consumers: Wade Farms and Walmart have no corporate relationship. It would be an astounding coincidence that two managers in two different locations were each digging into their own pockets to mail me cash, accompanied by what look like handwritten notes. Instead, it's just another way for companies to achieve a "We Care" effect without making the fundamental changes to improve their products. I'm not complaining, though. Cash is best, however it arrives.

CONSUMERISTS AND THE AMERICAN WAY

American corporations justify outsourcing as a way to satisfy consumer demand for lower prices. The buying masses have given their tacit approval of this corporate strategy by continuing to buy what's on the shelves at whatever price. I guess companies and regular consumers can afford to ignore collateral issues like Quality Fade. We consumerists can't.

Sure, we want to make a few bucks off the sorry state of things. But we're also in the vanguard of consumer culture.

We know the truth. We know prices should be even lower. Overseas labor is a fraction of the cost of comparable American labor. So why don't prices go way down?

Here's the rub: As manufacturing heads out of the United States, the **disemployment rate** rises and lower wages follow. Low prices are high for people without jobs or with jobs at lower salaries. QF is not so much a consequence of outsourcing or globalization as it is a shortsighted strategic decision to lower costs now, come what may later. Outsourcing may produce immediate savings, but its long-term consequences are damaging the American economy by condemning our manufacturing capacity to rust. We should be rebuilding to compete. We cannot change QF, but we can draw attention to it and profit from it.

THE VICIOUS SHORTSIGHTED CYCLE OF LOWER PRICES NOW

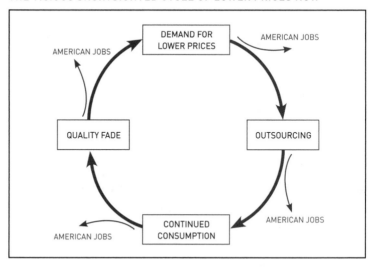

CHAPTER 5

FULFILLMENT FAILURE

Corporations avoid doling out compensation for a Fulfillment Failure (FF)—when what you order doesn't arrive—by blaming random chance, misunderstood promotional offers, even "acts of God." This last excuse helps people of faith accept bad weather, a delivery truck breakdown, or a GPS malfunction. Corporations are professional blame dodgers. If a corporation can get a consumer to accept that good intentions governed the non-delivery of a product or service, the corporate problem is solved at low cost.

A consumerist rejects this Failed Fulfillment folly. If a corporation is sending a consumer something—whether it's a big box or a message from a cloud—that corporation owns the process of delivery until the consumer takes possession. You are supposed to receive what you paid for when it was promised. No excuses.

Sometimes companies must concoct excuses for not sending an item at all. They try to obscure promises on delivery dates to head off later complaints about the actual number of days it took. You've probably noticed that fulfillment centers and their delivery outlets now begin the count with the next business day and sometimes only include weekdays. They offer Saturday or speedier service for an extravagant extra charge. They establish a date later than anticipated to lower expectations and, if the product arrives sooner, that makes the consumer happier.

CAUTIONARY TALES OF THE FULFILLMENT FIASCOS

Delivery Woes

"I'm out front with your package," said the driver in his truck parked curbside in a December snowstorm in New Jersey. He was calling from his cell phone. In his truck was a large box from a gallery in Indianapolis. In the box was a stone pedestal that weighed about 50 pounds. He had the invoice in his hand, asking me to come for my box. I had to sign for it.

"You are bringing the box inside our house, right?" I asked.

"Nope," said he, "this is a curbside delivery."

The driveway is long and steep. He had a hand truck. I did not. His plan was to convince me that his job was to unload the box at the curb, get my signature, and be off to his next stop. Unless, of course, I paid him extra for his added assistance. Invoices for heavy, expensive items usually specify delivery terms and conditions. If the delivery details are murky or non-existent, an entrepreneurial driver might try to pick up some extra bucks to bring it in. The curbside drop-off routine is one of many.

I'm sure the courier of my package had tried a few in his time. "Wait there," I said. "Or, better, come up to the house. It's warmer inside. I have to phone the gallery." The gal at the gallery said delivery terms were up to the courier service, not the gallery. I gave her a choice: "Tell the guy that delivery includes bringing it into the house, or that you'll pay him extra to get it done. Otherwise the next stop for the box is back where it came from. It's up to you. Here he is." I handed the driver the phone and within a few minutes the box was in the house. I offered the guy a cup of coffee.

My Free Kodak Printer Came at a Price

Amazon.com's attempt to deliver my new Kodak printer got off to a bad start. On its first try, Amazon's Midwestern fulfillment center crammed the printer into a shipping carton too small—picture shoving a sleeping bag into a poster tube. No cushioning material was in place for five of the six surfaces that needed to absorb the inevitable bumps and bounces between the fulfillment center and New Jersey.

The printer carton inside the shipping box arrived with all eight corners crushed. I contacted Amazon: Because the printer container did not arrive in perfect condition, the printer might develop problems. It had to have been hit and jostled severely. Take it back and try again. The center tried to get me to buy a shipping box suitable for the return trip. I threatened to call the charge card company and dispute the charge. Proper fulfillment is part of the deal.

Amazon has grown exceptionally large. Like all corporations that get this way, management loses touch with consumers and even its own operations in different states. It even loses touch with personnel on different floors of its headquarters. Amazon's Customer Service could not force Amazon's Fulfillment department to fulfill orders in any way other than how fulfillment management chose to operate: Ship without regard for the contents. The center finally agreed to ship me an empty, larger carton filled with plastic cushion bags for return of the first printer for full credit.

The second printer arrived in the same too-small box as the first. It did avoid the bumps and grinds that the first printer had endured—because part of the journey apparently was aboard a boat. A leaky boat. The upper half of the box was soaked.

Swaths of cello-tape applied after the watery mishap held it together. This time I asked Amazon to cancel the order and pick up the printer.

An Amazon specialist took charge. He instructed me to leave it outside my home where a UPS driver would pick it up. He gave me a five-day window. The days passed, the printer remained. I notified Amazon. My specialist said there had been a screwup and UPS would be there in a new one-to-five-day window. During that period, various UPS drivers delivered packages, often leaving them on top of the printer box. No paperwork, no pickup, and no charge for printer No. 2.

I stopped calling Amazon to say the printer had not been picked up. Since no new charge appeared for printer No. 2, I did the right thing from a consumerist perspective: I unpacked it, set it up, and figured, why tell Amazon? After all, I did my part giving the company feedback on its order-filling dysfunctionality. Amazon owed me. No charge for a $250 printer was only fair. Despite its waterlogged trip to my house, the printer worked just fine.

CONSUMERIST TIP: IS YOUR PACKAGE ACCEPTABLE?

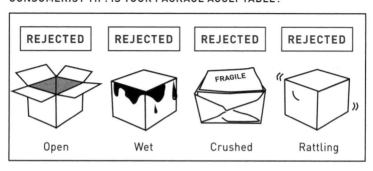

A Very Bergdorf Christmas

When a corporation like Bergdorf Goodman depends on another corporation like FedEx to fulfill its orders, the potential multiplies for two companies to pinch you at the same time. Remember my corporate pincer concept? (See page 30.) The probability of being a victim—or a victorious consumerist—rises exponentially during Christmas.

My family takes Christmas seriously. Gifts are central to Xmas's spiritual significance for us. Buying expensive clothes at steep discounts adds genuine joy to the season. Timing counts: The presents need to be fancily wrapped and under the tree by Christmas Eve. My wife really treasures on-sale couture from Fifth Avenue. The one problem is that items are sold as FINAL SALE/NO RETURNS. To avoid a bad purchase, my wife and I have an understanding. We wait until the mid-December sale discounts get serious. We start with a ridiculously pricey lunch, select the clothes together, have a few altered as needed, and have everything shipped from New York State to New Jersey to legally avoid New York State sales tax. When Christmas arrives, knowing what is in the boxes does not diminish the fun. Instead, it ensures happiness and eliminates the agony of returns.

In December 2008, the new recession had caught retailers like Bergdorf Goodman with too much expensive merchandise for too few buyers who still had money to spend. Discounts from 50% to 75% moved the inventory to near-reasonable levels.

We arrived at BG on December 12 at 1:00 p.m. We had a fabulous lunch at its seventh-floor café, which overlooks Central Park. Then the serious work began. We toured "on sale" racks throughout the store. We shopped for three hours, spurred on by complimentary wine and soda water. A roaming clerk took us for big spenders and led us from rack to rack, floor by floor. We stayed beyond closing time and lingered to watch a party on the fourth floor attended by the truly rich and famous. A good day. My wife bought eight items at an average 60% discount, some needing alterations at extra cost because they were on sale.

Delivery was promised for Tuesday (December 23) or Christmas Eve (December 24) at the latest. "No problem," assured the specially assigned salesperson who gave me her card. Commissions danced in her eyes like sugarplum fairies.

Sadly, when the going gets tough, FedEx gets confused. When things get busy, the back rooms of high-end clothing retailers do not run as efficiently as their showrooms. I called on Monday (December 22) to confirm shipment. Everything was on track, I was told. Nothing arrived on Tuesday morning (December 23), but BG convinced itself that the package was on the way because it had the FedEx tracking number. I was reassured that all was well and that I could track my package on the FedEx website. Besides, as BG had promised, if it did not arrive on Tuesday, it would for sure come on Wednesday.

Of course, it did not arrive on Wednesday.

By then, the planets were aligning themselves for an event made to order for a consumerist. BG employees were anxious to depart BG premises at exactly 5:00 p.m. on Wednesday to start their Christmas holiday. Based on conversations with BG employees present and still somewhat sober, they were sure the package would arrive before Wednesday was over. Bye-bye and Merry Christmas!

At 4:58 p.m. on Christmas Eve, BG stopped answering its phones. BG was going into lockdown mode. The Christmas selling season was officially over for them. At that moment, Christmas Eve delivery looked hopeless. I left a message at 5:01 p.m. on December 24: *You probably ruined our Christmas. You chose FedEx for fulfillment. Thanks to them, you may get the whole purchase back because you breached the contract between us. "No-return" implies having something to return.*

That particular Christmas Eve day, FedEx's much lauded website (lauded by FedEx, that is) was overwhelmed and under-informed. Its capacity could not live up to FedEx's promise of reliability. (Later, FedEx representatives admitted that there had been system-wide problems.) Whatever was or was not happening was not showing up on its website. FedEx had said it was aware of what needed to go where. But that's like Air Traffic Control saying it knows where planes should go in the sky without actually seeing them on radar. Distance was not the problem: The package had to travel only 22 road miles, from New York City to our house in Montclair, New Jersey.

Each FedEx toll-free customer service person I spoke with on Christmas Eve confidently reported status updates. They sounded like bedtime stories made up at the moment of telling. Yet all were supposed to be based on what FedEx's tracking system said. Each service rep was sure:

- The package would arrive at our home by 10:00 p.m. Christmas Eve because FedEx was working until midnight. (Untrue.)
- It was at Newark Liberty International Airport where I could pick it up if I drove there and asked for Fred. (Not going to happen.)
- There were *two* packages, not one. This was true and it was the only time the FedEx system had a useful connection

to truth. (BG had given me one tracking number and missed the second one.)
- The packages would be available if I went to the FedEx *Clifton*, New Jersey, facility between 8:00 a.m. and noon Christmas morning. (Wrong location.)

Now it was Christmas. No packages. No joy. Grumpy guerrilla consumerist.

Based on past FedEx fulfillment fiascos, I guessed that if the boxes went anywhere, they were probably at the FedEx *Fairfield*, New Jersey pickup location. I got through to John, the Clifton FedEx manager, who arranged for the delivery of both packages to our home at 1:19 p.m. on Christmas Day. The FedEx driver cheerily added, "Merry Christmas!" It would get merrier after the holiday.

Let's recount: I wasted time tracking the untrackable. We had a giftless Christmas morning. And that wasn't all; one of the dresses arrived with a stain on it that was not present when we purchased it. BG backroom mishandling, no doubt about it. When BG reopened the day after Christmas, a manager called. In summary, her reactions to my message left on Christmas Eve and another one on Christmas Day:
- Bring back the stained dress. We found a replacement. There will be no charge for the new one and the charge for the stained one is canceled. ($538)
- All the alteration charges are canceled. ($180)
- Shipping charges are canceled. ($18.50)
- Be our guests for lunch at Bergdorf's. When you make your reservation, ask for the manager. He will be expecting you. (Lunch there is about $150 per couple without champagne.) "OK?" she asked.

```
************************************
STAINED DRESS CREDIT           538.00

ALTERATION CHARGES CREDIT      180.00

SHIPPING CHARGES CREDIT         18.50

BG LUNCH (@ 2 PERSONS)         300.00

CHAMPAGNE                       A LOT

TOTAL                      $1,036.50+

************************************

          THANK YOU, WE VALUE
            YOUR PATRONAGE
```

"OK," I said. We got the champagne free, too, poured by the manager. I lost count of how many flutes I drank, so the value is not included.

Escada Eventually Got It Right

The first time Escada shipped a clothing purchase to Virginia instead of New Jersey, UPS held it in Virginia for us to pick it up from New Jersey. I have never lived or been arrested in Virginia. I have no idea how the confusion came about. For sure, I wasn't driving 500 miles round-trip to correct someone else's blunder. We told UPS to just ship it to us. UPS held firm: Escada had somehow changed our address on the order. UPS sent it there and held it there. That's the way the carrier's system worked. Escada was aware of the problem, but was powerless to correct it.

Presumably, UPS worked for Escada—at least that is the way I saw it. This was a pincer moment: I was getting squeezed between the incompatible systems of two corporations. The package eventually reached us. Not on time. Not to my satisfaction. Mismanagement is an exploitable weakness that I let them get away with.

I didn't let the chance go by the second time Escada shipped a clothing purchase to Virginia. That was in 2006. My wife and I had bought the Escada clothing at a 60% discount during an early pre-Christmas sale. When I paid, I emphasized two requirements: First, the goods must arrive in New Jersey no later than "next Thursday" because we were flying early the next day, Friday morning, to Miami, where my wife planned to wear the new clothes. Second, make sure our address is in New Jersey, not Virginia. Not to worry, Escada said, everything is under control. The delivery will arrive on Tuesday, plenty early.

When nothing came on Tuesday, I alerted Escada. The representative suggested that I use the "Track It Yourself" feature on the UPS website. Consumerists know better than to take charge of their own abuse; I said Escada was the sender and must be the enforcer. Escada called back to assure us that it would arrive on Wednesday.

On Wednesday afternoon, UPS reported good news and bad news. First, the good news: The package was delivered. The bad news: It was delivered to Virginia again. I tried to look at the good news part. Delivery to Virginia was better than to Holland or Guatemala. I made a suggestion to Michael, the Escada manager: UPS works for you! *Command* UPS to expedite the expeditable: Overnight the package to get to me by Thursday, easy to do at just 250 miles away. He promised he would get the package to arrive Thursday. An image of Michael started to form: He is standing at the edge of the Atlantic Ocean. He commands the tide to reverse course.

To his credit, by Thursday Michael had moved the package much closer: It was in New Jersey at a UPS facility. However, Michael admitted that he could not get UPS to deliver the package to our house until Friday. I asked, "At the airport entrance, perhaps, before we take off?"

Michael had an alternative. Maybe UPS could deliver it on Friday to our hotel in Miami? That way my wife's clothes would be there before we arrived.

Michael, Michael! To inject a third corporation—the hotel—into the picture would be the makings of the perfect fulfillment storm. Trusting UPS and the hotel to have my wife's clothes there, as promised, could allow her to pack almost nothing for the trip to Miami. But what if they couldn't deliver and she had no clothes to wear for her meeting? Michael, do you want to deal with that?

I had a more sensible plan—much easier to implement than getting UPS to do anything out of the ordinary: Ask the pilot of our Continental flight from Newark to make an unscheduled stop at the UPS facility in New Jersey. I also told Michael that Escada is about to lose a client and he could cancel the purchase.

Michael asked for more time. He called back: Escada values our business and will issue a charge card credit for half the purchase price. The credit went to our credit card a few hours later. The package arrived the following week. My wife wore something else to her meeting in Miami. The compensation totaled $2,692—well worth the inconvenience.

CONSUMERIST TIP: ACCEPTABLE DELIVERY

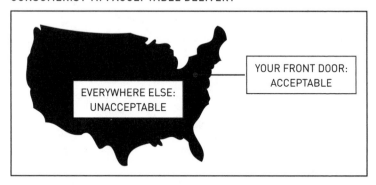

YOUR FRONT DOOR:
ACCEPTABLE

EVERYWHERE ELSE:
UNACCEPTABLE

All the News That's Fit to Soak

The *New York Times* has reporters and editors who excel at bringing readers in-depth news coverage of the country and the world. It just doesn't know how to deliver a dry paper on a wet day. The delivery service wraps the paper in blue plastic and delivers it before the sun comes up.

The problem is the critical last stage of fulfillment: delivering the paper intact and fully legible in a spot that is convenient for the customer to pick it up. Sometimes I find the paper in the street. Sometimes it comes to rest on the sidewalk and is taken by news-junkie joggers. It can get wedged under a hedge and not be discovered for days. Ours often lands on the driveway, where the mail truck runs it over, leaving tread marks that make it hard to read. I can deal with that. What really chafes my consumerist psyche is the driveway delivery during morning rains or before-dawn sprinklers. The blue wrap holds the water.

Goldfish have a better chance of surviving in the newspaper than I have of reading it.

Incidentally, I take care of my delivery people. I give cash at Christmas to newspaper carriers and my postal carrier. I offer UPS and FedEx drivers hot drinks in cold weather and cool beverages on hot days. I do my part to encourage them to do theirs.

Even in the Internet age, life in the suburbs depends on home delivery of newspapers. I can't point, click, read, scroll, and sip my coffee at the same time. I want my news on paper. I want the paper to be dry. Whenever a paper is damaged, I call the toll-free number and get an automatic credit. It takes thirty seconds. If I have to buy a replacement at its retail cost, I connect to an operator to get the full price credited. If I experience a run of papers delivered on the sidewalk or the street, I call to get a refund or a free subscription extension. My complaints stimulate better delivery for a while. In any year my compensation for poor delivery nets me between $20 and $30. Sometimes a lot more.

The *Financial Times*, the London-based business daily, is a relative newcomer to the shrinking newspaper industry. In the beginning, its delivery was about as consistent as the Dow Jones Industrial Average. It shares delivery service in New Jersey with the *New York Times*. When the delivery of either is botched, I pounce on both publications for refunds. I'm a consumerist. I like profiting by killing two birds with one stone.

In 2007, the *Financial Times* extended my subscription three months because of delivery problems. It was upgrading its support systems by downgrading customer service into various do-it-yourself options. Mishaps continued. The *FT* gave me a free six-month subscription extension in 2008 (about $175).

Occasionally the *New York Times* has done likewise. Both newspapers keep records of past complaints. It speeds up resolution of new complaints and reduces the time I need to explain my requests for compensation.

In the spring of 2009, the *Financial Times* came up with a deal to deliver its content in a slick online format at an introductory price of $1.82 a week for one year. I tried to order it online, but the *FT* system failed. I tried the *FT* toll-free number. Service reps had not heard about the offer. I explained it to them. As it turned out, *FT* marketing had not told *FT* circulation. A supervisor gave me a complimentary one-year online subscription, worth about $200.

Why are newspaper publishers concerned about delivery fulfillment and consumer satisfaction? Because they are concerned about advertisers. The *New York Times* can speak for itself on this matter: Its 2009 annual report stated, "We have powerful and trusted brands whose relevance and high-quality content attract educated, affluent and influential audiences highly valued by advertisers."[15] They need readers to keep advertisers and they know it.

Newspaper ad revenues are falling in proportion to consumers' expanded use of cable news and web news. Subscription revenues are a smaller source of income than advertising revenues. But they are directly related. So newspapers will pay in response to legitimate complaints to hold onto customers. We are worth every dollar of compensation. From 2007 to 2009, the *Financial Times* and the *New York Times* paid me $650 for their fulfillment failures. That's certainly fulfilling for a news-hungry consumerist.

CHAPTER 6

CUSTOMER DISSERVICE

SECTION ONE: WHERE WE ARE

"On the one hand, C.E.O.s routinely describe service as essential to success. On the other hand, customer service is a classic example of what businessmen call a 'cost center'—a division that piles up expenses without bringing in revenue," writes James Surowiecki in the *New Yorker*. "Most companies see it as tangential to their core business, something they have to do rather than something they want to do."[16]

The long-term goal of Customer Service is to morph into consumer self-service. It's a new twist on the "Pull yourself up by your own bootstraps" idea. At this writing, corporations are halfway there. Toll-free lines begin with prerecorded phrases about delays in answering calls due to heavy call volume, recent changes in menus, and how much better service would be if you simply hung up now and used the website. The lengthy description of which number to press is my personal favorite. I always choose the one most likely to get me to a real person. Then I explain that I am ill and do not think I have the strength to dial all over again, so may I please be connected to the right place.

Corporations understand that behavioral changes in consumers take time. The cost of Customer Service has the attention of corporate leaders. But rather than reduce service blunders, corporations reduce service. The ripple effect can reach as far as Bangalore, India.

The Buddies of Bangalore

I am not an Indiaphobe. However, I am a vigorous Bangalore-phobe. Thomas Friedman, the usually well-informed *New York Times* columnist and best-selling author, has praised Bangalore,

India, for its high-tech advances and personnel training. Evidently, Mr. Friedman has never dealt with Customer Service from the Buddies of Bangalore, a Covad Communications' outsource for technical support.

For years, Covad Communications, Inc., of San Jose, Calif., was AT&T's overflow support arm for AT&T's consumer DSL lines. Covad's strength is in the commercial rather than the consumer side of DSL services. Covad sub-outsourced to India and Canada.

Covad's Bangalore subcontractor took **abuse cluster** to a new level. AT&T exits and enters consumer services based on what is good for AT&T. Some of its services travel over cable telephone poles owned by AT&T. AT&T leases lines to competitors. That puts giant telecoms in the predicament of having to cooperate with each other while they battle each other, like an army asked to shoot at enemy forces during the day and sleep with them at night.

So it was that the AT&T cable carried a phone line leased to Verizon for our local service and another line for long distance. One pole, one cable, two phone lines, two telecoms. To complicate matters, both telecoms outsource customer service to distant places to cut costs.

Our local service Verizon line went dead one day in November 2009. We had to prove to Verizon that it was an "outside" problem (their responsibility) by unplugging all the phones; that proved the problem was not "inside" (our responsibility). Verizon sent a lineman to climb the AT&T pole and fix it. He inadvertently (we presume) knocked out our AT&T DSL line, also atop that pole in the cable. However, to make the same climb up the same pole again, Verizon must ask AT&T's permission, an action that cannot start until the consumer calls AT&T, and only then will they send an authorization for Verizon to climb the pole and "touch" the wire leased by Verizon from AT&T. The FCC enforces this procedure. (I have never seen any FCC agents. Maybe they observe the poles by spy satellite.)

The AT&T-to-Verizon mess started on a Thursday. I called AT&T to get it to contact Verizon. I called AT&T Customer Service a couple of times for an update. The calls automatically went to Covad Communications' subcontractor in Bangalore. Starting Thursday and through to Sunday night, the Bangaloreans issued apologies followed by variations dependent on which service person was issuing the assurance: The fix would happen within forty-five minutes. The fix will happen in twenty-four hours. They all agreed that the one vital enabling event had occurred: AT&T had sent the OK-to-climb message to Verizon. One Bangalorean said Verizon told her a guy was coming on Friday—so I must be there. Consumers must observe a time frame convenient to the telecom by answering service visit confirmation calls within three rings. Otherwise, the consumer is absent without telecom permission and the appointment is canceled without further notice.

When the Verizon lineman did not show up on Friday, Covad reported, "He was delayed" and I was to hang in there because he was coming soon. Around 7 p.m. Covad said, "So sorry, he will be there between 8 a.m. and 4 p.m. on Saturday." At 3 p.m. on Saturday, Covad assured me he'd be there within forty-five minutes. (Mr. Friedman, are you reading this?)

I tried Verizon. After all, its fingerprints were on the downed DSL line. The call went to Verizon's outsourced Customer Service Center in the Caribbean. An agent said no AT&T

authorization was in the system. The Verizon service person had a practical idea: If I could find a Verizon store with Sunday hours, I could buy a Verizon "air card" to plug into the computer to get the DSL service.

On Monday, AT&T finally sent the authorization to Verizon. (Would it be unfair to say Covad's Bangoloreans were not telling the truth?) Early Monday evening Verizon fixed the problem—although it took two climbs and four hours. Verizon had insisted that only a DSL-trained person could fix the problem on the pole. No one was available because DSL-trained people were scarce. (And it was a competitor's line?) Verizon turned at last to a non-DSL person who was the same guy who had fixed the Verizon line and disabled the AT&T line that started this saga.

Just when we thought we were done with Covad/Bangalore, four months later in March 2010, AT&T, with less than thirty days' advance warning, informed its consumers that AT&T DSL service was no longer available in our region. AT&T was dropping DSL service in the most populated metro area in America but not to worry, it would be an easy transition. The PR copy chirped:

> *Continue your Internet service with Covad in just 5 easy steps! Approximately 45 minutes to one hour after completing the Covad registration process, your Internet service will be transferred to Covad.*[17]

Covad and AT&T were as ready for the ensuing chaos as New Orleans was for Katrina. Thousands of distress calls flattened Covad's toll-free technical support in the USA, India, and Canada. Later a Covad executive admitted to me that AT&T "had let Covad down." It took a week to get our DSL service to work because incoming calls required thirty to forty minutes for online service assistance to answer, if it answered at all. The fixes turned out to be temporary until Covad figured out what to do.

DO-IT-YOURSELF CUSTOMER-SERVICE DAY PLANNER

DAY 1	DAY 2	DAY 3
Verizon service line goes dead. Prove it is their responsibility to send someone.	Verizon lineman climbs up the pole and fixes problem, knocking out AT&T DSL line.	Call AT&T to get authorization for Verizon to climb pole and "touch" the wire leased from AT&T.
DAY 4	**DAY 5**	**DAY 6**
Call AT&T to follow up. Your call goes to Covad's sub-contractor in Bangalore.	Get message from Bangalore that AT&T okayed Verizon to climb. Wait for lineman.	Get report from Covad that lineman was delayed and will come today. Wait for lineman.
DAY 7	**DAY 8**	**4 MONTHS LATER...**
Call Verizon's out-source center in the Caribbean to check in. Find out there was no AT&T authorization.	AT&T finally sends the authorization to Verizon; lineman climbs pole and fixes problem.	AT&T drops DSL service in your area and Covad takes over your internet service. **Start over again.**

I got compensated for the mishaps, although not in proportion to the time I spent to get service. Covad gave me three months of DSL at no charge (about $90). I've butted heads with Covad several times since then. Sometimes my beefs go to Covad managers in the good ol' USA because Covad's outsourced technical support focuses on commercial services, not on serving consumers like me. Covad has stuck with Bangalore. This is customer support, telecom style. Get used to it. Learn to profit from it.

SECTION TWO: FAUC YOU

The way customer service is headed, by 2018 only a few kinds of calls will be answered by operators—most likely for an additional charge. Corporations think consumers treat toll-free calling like an entitlement program, therefore the idea is to "migrate" consumers into paying for these calls. If corporations are going to provide toll-free numbers, consumers are going to have to pay for the calls.

As long as corporations pay up when they screw up, I'm all for globalization, outsourcing, automation, and robotization. Obviously outsourcing Customer Service to faraway places may lower costs, and the value for the consumer is mostly in acquiring more cultural awareness than in product or service assistance.

The suspicion grows that a plot is afoot to "evolve" the consumer to into Full Acceptance and Unquestioning Cooperation (FAUC) of Do-It-Yourself Problem Resolution (DIYPR).

The Implementation Model

Karl Marx would have loved the irony of what corporations are now up to: Move ever toward the goal of dumping Customer Service into a customer responsibility, but understanding that the process will at times make great progress followed by a small retreat. This corporate strategy for the staged changeover thus revitalizes the Marxist dialectic of "two steps forward, one step backward." Basically, the motto taught revolutionaries how to move toward a goal by taking a couple of big steps forward and, if the resistance was still standing, temporarily taking a small step backward. This means mistakes that victimize consumers become part of the process.

THE CORPORATE STRATEGY BOOGIE

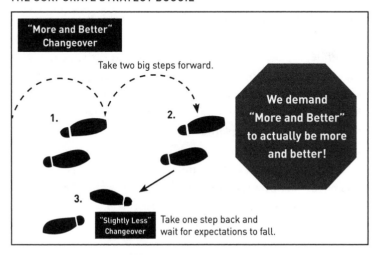

Reliance on extensively trained people with hands-on experience with the products and services is no longer realistic. It is hard to train employees to understand the inner workings of a wind-up alarm clock, let alone a sophisticated home computer. As products get smaller and become obsolete faster, personalized service will cost more than the product, even if service is outsourced to Bangalore. What's more, is it fair for customer service reps to have to deal with consumers who are hostile from the get-go? How would you like to hear a consumer begin a call, "I paid for perfection and this is not it," or "I am not happy about the music selections I had to listen to before you came on"? Customers deserve help, but they shouldn't mistreat service reps to get it.

I know my plea for mercy seems a little out of character. But being an effective consumerist also means knowing who *isn't* your enemy. Service reps are merely the messengers of bad tidings. They are facing tough times under a corporate attitude that puts profits before products. The more successful product lines proliferate, the faster "service amnesia" about earlier models develops. Service people may confuse old products with new products—and accidentally come up with solutions that would have solved problems for another product. That won't end.

Those who field complaints for a living—from Bakersfield to Bangalore—are caught in the middle. Manufacturing executives see no dollar signs in putting quality first. It's far less costly to let cheap labor handle the complaints, no matter how angry the caller. The top brass still collect their revenue.

CAN YOU SPOT THE ENEMY?

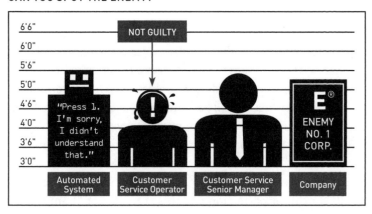

Too Expensive to Continue

Tech support can feel the squeeze, too. If a product is not selling well, a company decreases its resources to help consumers fix glitches. Less staff and shrinking enthusiasm to serve the consumer beget even more problems—and more avenues for the consumerist to exploit.

My ADT alarm system can be remotely turned on and off. When I needed to let someone into my home while I was 2,600 miles away, I turned off the system—or thought I did until the authorized person entered the home and set off a shrieking alarm. He couldn't hear the code I was shouting into the phone. We were interrupted by a call from ADT to tell me that my alarm had gone off. The chaos would not have occurred had I—and ADT—known that the remote turnoff worked only when activated by a landline phone, not the cell phone I had used. No one at ADT knew how the alarm worked because, as I discovered later, the product sold poorly, so no one cared much or could find anyone who did. I registered my complaint about the oversight, and ADT gave me a 50% reduction for six months' coverage, amounting to about $250.

The Fly in the Wine

Doctors once made house calls in America. The few who still do are mostly in movies and go to very wealthy patients. A few corporations also make house calls, usually under special circumstances. In 1970, I reported finding a fly in a bottle of Almaden wine. The fly was well preserved in the bottle and available for viewing if Almaden wanted to see it. Damn if Almaden didn't take me up on the offer.

Almaden Vineyards, based in San Jose, Calif., sent Orey Facinni as its investigator. Apparently, Customer Service was a good place to break in a new guy who had recently emigrated from Italy; was unfamiliar with the quickest way to go the 20 miles from San Jose to Palo Alto, where we lived; and was frazzled by the traffic. All for a fly in a bottle.

He confirmed that there sure was a fly there. He was sorry about my distress. But his conclusion was the fly flew in *after* the bottle had left the distillery. I replied that I did not put or invite the fly in. It had gained entry *before* I opened the bottle. I also told Mr. Facinni that if I had chosen a wine bottle in which to plunk a dead fly, it would have been an expensive one, not this cheapo half-bottle under investigation.

The assertion energized Facinni into a verbal and physical reenactment of Almaden's überhygienic bottling conditions: He made circles with his arms to represent the conveyor rotating with hundreds of bottles, each stopping to be mechanically filled, corked, and sealed. It was performance art of a rare caliber. He depicted the wine bottle with his right hand in a fist, then used a finger of his left to cork the bottle. To act out the final plastic seal, he clasped his hands together. It left us breathless.

Impressed but not convinced, I told him his performance simply proved that I was right. The wine bottle is *momentarily open* between the wine fill and cork insertion. I had seen it firsthand because I had been on the Almaden tour. "That is when it must have happened, Mr. Facinni. Just enough time for a fly to dive into a bottle."

Facinni stared at me. He left the house. He returned with a case of full-size bottles as Almaden's gift to me for my time and trouble. He asked for directions to get to San Jose. The case was worth then about $80 (after the usual 10% discount for a case). That's about $460 in 2011. However, Almaden wine has not risen in value at that rate. These days a case of wine as good or better than that Almaden is $80 to $120. The case I got as comp is worth about $100 in wine these days, but I still toast my victory and Mr. Facinni's performance.

SECTION THREE: THECORPORATION

The means by which corporations disservice consumers are not accidents, nor are they haphazard. They are thought-out, methodical tactics that serve the sole purpose of increasing profitably in almost complete disregard to consumer satisfaction. The modicum of care they do have for satisfaction is a result of their need to retain consumers and not send all of them running for the hills. Corporations seek the perfect balance between the bare minimum cost they can expend and still maintain the facade of Customer Service. In their efforts to keep the amount of money they have to shell out to run Customer Service and compensate dissatisfied consumers to that minimum, they induce hold times long enough to watch *Gone with the Wind*, they invent labyrinths of departments through which to shuffle the handful of patient callers that make it to a representative, and they try their very best to send consumers to inscrutable FAQ sites where they can burnout on frustration alone.

Below is my take on what an honest report of the processes and progresses of a Customer Service department in any corporation would like. Though "TheCorporation" and its employees are not real, the tactics they use and the tack they take certainly are.

TO: Officers and Directors of TheCorporation

RE: Annual Customer Service Group Report

FROM: Director, Customer Service Group (CSG)

EXECUTIVE SUMMARY

For the third consecutive year, CSG has registered significant productivity gains as measured by the Seven Key Indicators Package (SKIP):

1. **Toll-Free Complaints Incoming:** 27% increase to 3,476,212 calls.

2. **Toll-Free Calls Actually Answered:** 22% reduction.

3. **Net Efficiency Gain:** 49% (27% increase incoming with 22% reduction live-op involvement).

4. **Complaints Resolved:** 92%. Measured by complainants either not calling back after hanging up on automatic operators or abandonment before speaking to anybody.

5. **Web Utilization:** 24.5% increase. Measured by visits to website FAQs.

6. **Go-Away Payoffs:** 14.3% reduction in costs to pay consumers to go away. Substitution of HPVIs (High Perceived Value Items), such as coupons and credits to reduce costs of future purchases, instead of refund checks.

7. **Attempts to Contact TheCorporation:** 16.2% reduction. Phase-in plan to discourage contact with executive offices is in accelerated stage: Letters are not answered unless a form letter exists for that

purpose; operators deny knowledge of names and addresses or corporate locations or personnel and provide only their first name, rank, and op-number.

OPERATIONAL REVIEW

If we build a Customer Service operation, customers will come. Our long-term success will depend on how well we get them to prefer our automated services instead of our non-automated services.

Mission: Maximize customer satisfaction and minimize corporate cost. By definition, a customer who comes to CSG is not completely satisfied. The CSG job is to turn that customer once again into a "satisfied customer," one who CSG does not hear from again.

Tools of the Trade: CSG innovates twenty-first-century techniques for data gathering, customer expectation modification, and exploitation of underutilized sales opportunities.

Measures of Success: Caller abandonment rate, maximum perceived value of coupons by hard-to-please consumers, and construction of better barriers for access to non-automated support.

CSG Profit Center Progress: Costs have been reduced by 16.3%. Major factors were (a) outsourcing toll-free number reception to start-ups in the Caribbean and India and (b) sales training of service operators. Projected to reach break-even point by end of current FY [fiscal year].

CHANGING CUSTOMER PATHWAYS TO THE CORPORATION

Customers attempt to reach us by our toll-free numbers, websites, e-mail addresses, and standard mail. Direct communication with our Non-Automated Operators (NAOs) is limited to times and situations of our choosing.

CSG continues to develop and implement techniques that not only lead consumers to instructive **DIY** solutions everywhere they look, we supply an environment that encourages consumers to be happy in their quests for solutions. For instance, our music selection offers choices of classical, rock, and spiritual hymns during toll-free-number hang times. Our website offers links to other sites as well as to eighteen separate and distinct FAQs, based on the answers to questions asked after the call is auto-answered.

Operational protocols require NAOs to deny knowledge of corporate locations as well as their own. If asked, they explain it is for "security reasons." CSG NAOs volunteer a first name as supplied by us. The recent outsource locations in Uzbekistan use Karl or Katerina, those in Bangalore use Harris or Harriet, and the Canadians use Tom or Tam. E-mails sent by CSG inform customers that no responses can be made to our e-mails. E-mails that threaten violence are turned over to the FBI. (The number of threats has remained steady at 18%.) All CSG promotional literature and correspondence omit return mailing addresses, contact phone numbers, or names of key people.

The CSG menu has a new recorded message that offers eight prerecorded options, the last of which is to repeat the first seven. If complainants prematurely press "0" to speak to an operator or technical person, the system switches to the Ring Busy mode. The system does not permit transfer to any choices until after all choices are read (67 seconds). After a choice is made, the system auto-updates to predict length of wait time needed with a suggestion to try our website. (Note: During the recent salmonella panic, CSG added the words *really, really* to modify *important* in the standard *Your call is important to us and will hopefully be answered by the next available operator within the next 00 minutes. You may now choose your preferred music selection by pressing 7.*)

When calls are transferred to NAOs, they see a sales options screen with "best bets" to indicate product or service based on caller demographics and/or product for which service is being sought.

CUSTOMER AS COMPLAINANT

The Customer is hardly ever right. Customers who complain usually complain about the wrong thing. Although we know they are not right, we begin by feeling their pain without promising a cure. The doctor wants to keep the patient's business, has other patients waiting, and tries to think of offering free samples left by a salesman.

When we first encounter a complainant, we **triage** the situation in terms of what is good or not good for TheCorporation and into which slot the caller fits, or what we call Complainant Categorization (CC).

Neurotics (roughly 60%) have preexisting neuroses at the root of their product or service problems. The danger is they may yet find a way to reach an NAO. Their underlying problem is subconsciously blamed on our product or service, which was otherwise working as well as a *reasonable and healthy person* would expect. CSG allows enough time (3 minutes) for a cool-down to occur. During that period, although we are not therapists, we utilize time-proven therapies: Begin with profuse apologies wrapped in a calm demeanor. Assure the troubled complainant that we are feeling his/her pain and will try to help. (We stay vague about what that help involves.) We are doing these people an enormous favor by providing therapy long overdue. If that does not work, we place callers on hold for several minutes so that "the tincture of time" might do its magic work and the complainant will end the call and get on with his/her life.

If that does not work and the complainant is still on the line, the Tactical Options (shown in *Illustration #1—Tactical Options Chart* at the end of this report) are brought into play. CSG knows some people are just lonely and seek conversation, but these callers fail to appreciate how many others are waiting to be served.

Maximizers (30% of callers) start with grandiose expectations: They watch TV commercials heavy on promotional huff-and-puff, think fantasy novels are documentaries, and go to movies released during the summer. They believe they can buy something complicated, just remove it from its container, plug it in, and start using it.

Maximizers have the delusion that they live in a perfect world in which all products and services will work perfectly for as long as they own them—and that technical specialists have previously used a product or service and know the whereabouts of the technical manual. CSG's job is to gently dispel maximizers' unrealistic expectations and, if a quick fix is not available, leave the impression that someday soon it will be.

Our NAOs are trained to listen and equipped to look for opportunities to upgrade maximizers by selling them a replacement product or an extended service program. The bonus plan for turning service calls into sales opportunities has incentivized NAOs into working overtime. Well-received is the NAO-of-the-Month Award (NAOOTMA). It adds $50 to the commissions.

Deadbeats (10%) are a small consumer group with a criminal mentality. They will use any means for personal gain: Lie, cheat, mislead, and avoid paying interest fees or late charges for credit card purchases. They should not be confused with the neurotics or maximizers. As their stories unfold, our experienced customer service professionals see them as the ultimate challenge, the vandals at the door.

An instant indicator is Grievance Exaggeration (GE). Threats to contact consumer agencies, newspapers, and regulatory agencies are common among deadbeats. All of this is the send-up for an inflated and preposterous demand for compensation.

CSG is TheCorporation's first line of defense against these predators. We listen long enough to determine whether we recognize any item already on TheCorporation's defect list. If so, *Illustration #2—The Chart of Last Resort* (at the end of this report) is the most efficient answer.

CSG MENTALITY

Allegiance Transfer Syndrome (ATS) is a condition in which a customer service agent transfers allegiance from the corporation to the caller. Most often it occurs when a relatively new operator succumbs to the clever manipulations of a ruthless, hardened complainant. We monitor and record conversations for training and quality purposes. Rare instances of ATS are played back as a reminder to all operators of how a cleverly imagined story can cloud the mind of even a seasoned CSG veteran. Nevertheless, if this were a military situation, ATS would be tantamount to treason. Prevention is the best cure for ATS. At the start of each shift, operators recite the corporate pledge and are periodically reminded who they work for and why.

Big Picture Thinking (BPT) means having a total CSG commitment to becoming a profit center. We pledge to practice restraint in how to make each and every customer satisfied. Unless we do our part, TheCorporation will not reach its full potential. On that note we submit our annual report.

Illustration #1: **TACTICAL OPTIONS CHART**

TACTICAL OPTIONS In Order of Escalation	SCRIPTS
1. Go to Our Website	Try our website! It can answer all of your questions. It has pull-down windows to get instruction manuals you can print. Be sure to have plenty of paper in your printer. Go to **www.thecorporation.corp/selfhelp/diy/ productsservices.com**
2. Talk to a Specialist	I will now transfer you to a Technical Specialist who can offer more information than I have. Once connected, the system will ask you for some information that may be similar to what you have already given us. Wait until you hear all the options and you are prompted to make a selection. Then pick the specialist who sounds best.
3. Try to Talk to a Supervisor	I will now try to transfer you to my supervisor. He/she is very busy at the moment. If you have to be on hold, there are many pleasing works of music for you to listen to. Do you prefer popular or classic?
4. Transfer to a Mythical Location	I truly wish I could be of more assistance. I am going to transfer your call to another location that may be able to solve your problem. [Call goes to 10 minutes of music and suggestions to go to the website or call back on another day. Terminates automatically.]
5. Red Button	I really think you need to calm down. I am worried about you. Please call back when you can calmly state your problem. Good-bye— and good luck. [Push terminate call button.]

Illustration #2: **CHART OF LAST RESORT**

OFFER	CSG ACTION	TheCorporation BENEFIT
1. Exchange Level A	Replacement with same product.	Perceived value is greater than the actual value.
2. Exchange Level B	Replacement with a better product. *Requires escalation.*	Greater perceived value than Level A.
3. Coupon	Mail coupon for free product.	Perceived value is greater than cost of product with additional benefit to corporation because many coupons expire or are never redeemed.
4. Cash	Mail check or cash as the final solution. *Requires escalation.*	Only justified if complainant has credible case that will consume time and may be lost in a formal channel.
5. Extension	Add time to a service contract.	Retains customer at low risk to corporation—unless product or service is faulty.
6. Add New Service	Add new service to an established relationship.	Strengthens long-term relationship with complainant and presents opportunity to charge for services in the future.
7. Points	Add points to existing frequent-user account.	Points are cheap and can be hard to utilize.
8. Combo	Combine two or more of the above.	
9. Waive Fees	Interest and late payment charges, specific fees for services or membership .	High perceived value. *Note:* Avoid waiving fees.

PART 2

FIGHTING BACK THE RIGHT WAY—GET THE CASH

The next two chapters are this book's raison d'être. You are going to learn how to get the compensation you deserve for crappy products, crappy delivery, and crappy excuses. This is where the battle begins. Chapter 7 explores the enemy's mind-set and organizing principles. Chapter 8 provides the Weapons of Management Destruction. As guerrillas, we adopt what the enemy does to make the enemy pay. Our way has the advantages of efficiency, effectiveness, and irony. Never underestimate the power of irony.

CONSUMERIST CODE OF CONDUCT

The best guerrillas are guided by high moral principles. Or at least profitable ones.

- Consumerists should treat corporations the way corporations treat consumers. Do unto them when they do unto you.
- Consumerists have high expectations: Expect products and services advertised as perfect to be perfect. If you get anything less than perfection, attack.
- A consumerist's time is as valuable as a corporate executive's time.
- Consumerist complaints should be as creative as a corporation's promotion of a product or service.
- A consumerist's bottom line is as important as a corporation's bottom line.

SPIRITUAL GUIDANCE

A word about maintaining high ethics in dealing with corporations: Ugh.

Corporations want you to take the high moral ground while they play fast and loose with their manufacturing and promotion. As long as you play fair, they win. Every time. We won't tell lies—as soon as they stop telling lies. We'll exaggerate our comp claims as long as they exaggerate the effectiveness of their products.

Our outlook is their outlook: Growth. Profitability. Results. The end justifies the means. And why should corporations object to our strategy? They invented it. We are simply going to use it right back at 'em.

CHAPTER 7

KNOW THE ENEMY'S MIND AND TACTICS

A corporation is deceptively packaged as a living, thinking, caring entity. I want you to see a corporation for what it is: a collection of powerful people who will do anything to squeeze out more revenue. They will blame everybody and everything but themselves. They exploit tax loopholes big enough to drive a Hummer through. When they actually pay compensation for wrongdoing, they deny it is compensation.

Corporations are particularly adept at convincing gypped consumers that they are in the wrong, that it is they who owe the corporation. I've experienced this going back to ancient times—the 1960s.

PORTRAIT OF THE AUTHOR AS A DEADBEAT

Banks don't mind when they make mistakes, as long as the solution comes out in their favor. Your mission is to stand your ground. Maintain a steady stream of communication to document their idiocy. Maybe Crocker Bank thought it had a lamb as a customer when it messed with me. It should have known better: It was the late 1960s and people were no longer accepting the world as it was. Credit cards were becoming popular with their seductive promise of acquire now, pay later. I had a credit card issued by Crocker Bank. A monthly statement arrived one day with a charge for a $35 purchase made by one Leon Wisongrad that appeared on my statement for $124. A double whammy of a mix-up—I was getting ripped off twice! If Leon was trying to get me to pay for his charge, he should have signed my name instead of his, even though he had made the charge with his own credit card.

My sole connection with Leon was our Crocker Bank credit cards. At that time monthly statements were mailed along with carbon copies of the past month's transactions. The tissue amounts were supposed to equal the month's new charges. With or without Leon's $35 charge, the $124 exceeded any tissue combination sent to me. Without enclosing any payment, I sent the statement and a copy of Leon's tissue with an attached note:

This month's balance is more than the total of my tissues that came with the statement—even when I subtract the enclosed tissue from Leon Wisongrad, a guy I don't know well enough to pay his bills. Do you think he is a friend of mine? So I am not paying anything until you fix the mess you created. I hope you'll get on this real fast—like before next month's statement is made up.

The following month's statement was for about $25 worth of new charges I had made—with no Wisongrad tissues. There was an interest charge on the entire amount of the previous month's total balance.

I tried a different approach to get Crocker's attention. No payment again, just another attempt to make Crocker do its job:

Read the letter I sent last month. It explains why I am not making any more payments until you get this account straightened out. As for interest charges, forget them: I pay in full each month (when the balance is correct). But I will not pay Leon's bill. Not only have Leon and I not been formally introduced, he might have returned what he bought and taken the credit. (And why would he tell me?) Speaking of Leon, I am glad none of his tissues were enclosed. Did you send them to someone else? Are you sending my tissues to Leon? It seems only fair.

The next regular bill arrived with interest growing, fertilized by the high rate triggered by partial payments—plus the credit card business's special source of profitability: The Late Fee.

Credit card companies use the Late Fee as a nearly cost-free source of income and as a future negotiating tool. The fee is a fixed round number, a corporate version of the flat tax that electronically slips in when a payment does not officially arrive on time, according to the bank's way of keeping track of time. If a consumer disputes the fee with a good argument, the bank or credit card processor will drop the fee as a show of good will. An effective way to encourage fee cancellation is to simply declare, "Here's the deal: Drop the damn fee or close the damn account. You choose."

Consumerists should not take the rules and penalties concocted by financial people too seriously. They are mostly sound and fury signifying nothing. In 2010, the Federal Reserve Board capped most late-payment fees at $25. In the 1960s and 1970s, credit cards printed stern warnings on the back, like "Do not tear, bend, staple, or mutilate this card" with a reminder that the credit card was the *property* of the issuing entity. The industry may have abandoned that warning because of my next move with Crocker: I cut *and* stapled the card. If that is not card mutilation, what is? I added a note:

> *Goddamn it, until you read my past messages and get my account straightened out, NO PAYMENTS. As for the interest and late payment stuff, give them to Wisongrad, if he even exists. Really, I think you invented him. How do you like what I did to your card?*

I stopped using the account, thereby having an extended interest-free loan from Crocker. Another month passed. Crocker finally responded by having Linda Mojica write me a short personal letter telling me that she would investigate the mess. The letter would have arrived sooner had Linda gotten my street name and house number closer to the correct words and numbers. There were also incomplete sentences, grammatical errors, and misspellings of my name on the envelope and in the letter. Due to the circuitous trip back through the U.S. Postal Service, it arrived tattered and torn. Poor Linda. She was stuck with a consumer who was then a college English teacher. With my red ink pen, I corrected all the errors, gave it a gift grade of D+ (so as not to discourage her) and mailed it back to Crocker with a progress report:

> *I have figured out what is wrong. It is not the Linda Mojicas that you have hired, it's the lack of training you have provided. No wonder Crocker cannot figure out what I owe. If you cannot teach her to write a coherent letter or mail it to the right address, what hope is there of getting a correct balance, since math is harder than English? By the way, how is Leon?*

More time passed. Statements arrived each month. Interest charges mounted. Late fees proliferated. Dark warnings about the future of my credit rating were issued.

Crocker left me no choice. I applied my skills to figure out what was owed and what was not. I assembled all unpaid tissues. I subtracted the interest and penalties, and had a true total of $124 ($865 adjusted to 2011 dollars). My note to Crocker detailed the amount of the tissues, the number of times I had tried to alert the bank to its own problems, and of my Correction

Fee for the work I had done. I calculated that my time was worth $24/hour ($163 in 2011). Subtracting my fee from the balance, I offered but did not send Crocker $100 as full and final payment.

More time passed. Statements kept on coming with the usual penalties and threats and balance increases. One evening I got a call from Mr. Prince of Crocker Bank. His voice was professional, his style as smooth as silk:

"Mr. Selden, first I must apologize on behalf of the Crocker Bank. You have been treated badly. I have examined all of the correspondence and want you to know that it should never have gotten this far. The interest charges have been canceled, the late fees are gone. You owe us $124."

"Did you read my last letter?" I replied.

"Certainly, that is why I am calling."

"What about my fee?"

"Mr. Selden," said Mr. Prince, "The Crocker Bank does not pay its customers. Its customers pay the Crocker Bank."

"Does Crocker Bank pay Linda Mojica?"

"Of course. She is an employee."

"You saw the kind of work she does. You saw the sort of work I do. I charge more than you pay her—but quality costs."

"Mr. Selden, we are willing to settle this matter without the interest and penalties. Simply send me a check for $124."

"Nope. If you hadn't sent me Leon's tissue and had added up the total right at the start, none of this would have happened—including my time in figuring it out for you."

"Mr. Selden . . ."

"Mr. Prince. I am keeping track of the time for this call. I will add more if we keep talking."

"Mr. Selden, please send the payment to my attention."
Mr. Prince quickly hung up.

I sent a check for $100 to Crocker, writing *Full and Final Payment* in the area for payee endorsement. I sent it in the return envelope without Prince's name on it. Why make it easy?

The story did not end there.

Sequel#1: A Crocker statement arrived showing the $100 payment and cancellation of late fees and interest. Another line showed a $24 *Adjustment*. Crocker lawyers liked *adjustment* better than *fee*. Fee might indicate that it actually acquiesced to my charge for time and trouble.

Sequel #2: Several months later I saw a full-page Crocker ad in the *San Francisco Chronicle*. There was an ad featuring a large picture of Linda Mojica! The copy said people like Linda were Crocker's future. I believe my assistance with her grammar and spelling helped propel her advancement.

Sequel #3: Unsolicited, a new Crocker Bank VISA credit card arrived. To reward my "solid record and credit worthiness," it increased my credit limit.

THE CONSUMERIST'S ARSENAL

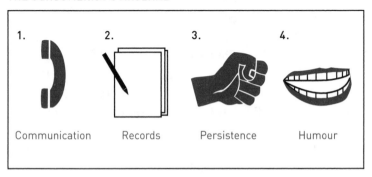

| 1. Communication | 2. Records | 3. Persistence | 4. Humour |

DISSATISFACTION MANAGEMENT (DM)

Corporations are not interested in *consumer satisfaction* as much as they are in *consumer dissatisfaction*. Forget their promotional claims. A satisfied customer is one they never hear from or who stays loyal to the brand even if the brand is disloyal to the consumer. Rather than work to keep customers satisfied, corporations spend more time and money figuring out how to manage the dissatisfied ones.

Dissatisfaction Management is designed to deter, derail, and defeat complaints. A smart manager builds defenses to anticipate and outsmart the majority of dissatisfied consumers. DM professionals utilize websites and mazelike phone networks to make complainants "disappear." DMs regularly meet and share war stories. They aim to put off the many and pay off the few. Your goal as a consumerist is to become part of the few.

Every business needs a dynamic strategy to keep executives on their toes as they observe competition, adjust to regulation, and plot ad campaigns. Consumer satisfaction is an afterthought.

Industries like to borrow tactics from outside sources, even the Mob. The main difference between organized crime and legitimate corporations is that organized crime breaks existing laws while legitimate corporations do things that ought to be against the law.

Consider Woody Allen's take on the convergence of Mob and corporate America's business strategy: "It is no secret that organized crime in America takes in over $40 billion a year. This is quite a profitable sum, especially when one considers that the Mafia spends very little for office supplies."[18]

Rigging is the financial services industry's insider term for how a bond rating corporation rigs a bond rating to please the bond issuer, rather than informing the investor. It leads ordinary consumers to buy overrated bonds that are actually junk. There are rigging applications in the agricultural industry with labels describing foods as *organic* and distributors slapping labels on household items saying *certified*, but without definitions of the words or details about the process behind the claims.

The Mob uses rigging, too. It seems to work for them. The *Financial Times* said, "The Mafia collectively was Italy's biggest company, taking in $59 billion a year."[19] The *New York Times* reported that "organized crime accounted for 7% of [Italy's] gross domestic product—the single biggest segment [at] $127 billion."[20] An Italian Mafia family sent agents through the fallen Berlin Wall in 1989 to buy up anything they could at fire-sale prices from unemployed KGB operatives, the *Financial Times* reported.[21] Arms, enriched uranium to make nuclear bombs, cargo planes—you name it. Then the Mafia marked up the unauthorized, uninspected goods like scalpers at the Super Bowl, earning a windfall in the tens of billions. It was a move right out of the rigger's playbook, which the Mafia wrote, by the way.

An alert executive looks and learns from other business practices. You can learn, too. Marking up goods that aren't so good is a criminal act. A consumerist guerrilla makes the criminals pay.

THE CORPORATION'S ARSENAL

1.	2.	3.	4.
WOW!	Due to unusually high call volume...	(thumbs up)	$
Good Marketing	Hard-to-Get Customer Service	Rigging	Corporate Money

LIABILITY LIMITATION

In this war, liability is a hazard of doing business. Corporations try to avoid liability by dodging and weaving as best as their wool suits will allow. When an incoming consumer complaint looks credible and expensive, they might call the wrongdoing a standard industry practice. Simply explain why something happened to justify its having happened. "The customer did not answer the phone for the delivery by the third ring, so our subcontracted delivery service could not bring the package to the actual address. It's standard industry practice to wait no more than three rings."

The Guarantees and Warranties Thicket

Guarantees and warranties should lower a customer's expectations of how well a product will work. A guarantee of a product's effectiveness within a certain time before the corporation projects it to fall apart saves the corporation any bother about it.

Planned Obsolescence

This is a vital part of corporate liability limitation. Rather than have a part become a future liability while still under warranty, it makes corporate sense to exclude it from coverage and designate it as a profitable "normal wear and tear" replacement part (for which the consumer has to pay). This concept perhaps stretches back to when Roman chariot makers calculated that the wheels would go first. Then charioteers had to bring the chariot back in for new wheels (not covered by warranty). The strategy was perfected by GMC in the 1950s.

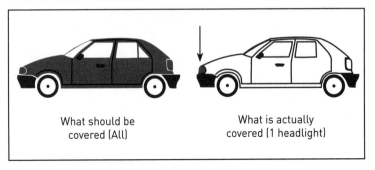

What should be
covered (All)

What is actually
covered (1 headlight)

Offer-Added Protection

Corporations that sell technology-dependent goods try to
profit from **extended warranty** or service agreements that end
when product deterioration is scheduled to begin. Their trick
is to sell consumers added protection just when they have
their credit card out to pay for a product at a cash register or
website. It works as a classic impulse buy. Executives know
that customers probably won't read the restrictive "Terms and
Conditions" and won't balk at the actual protection, which is
relatively modest.

No-Fly Frequent-Flier Points

Frequent-flier points are a bonanza for airlines, as long as
not too many points are redeemed for seats. Since FFPs are
a **contingent liability**, airlines give points as incentives to buy
tickets but take steps to restrict redemption. In an ideal world
for airlines, fliers will accumulate hundreds of thousands of
points but not use them for seats airlines could otherwise sell.
It is similar to the insurance industry's ideal world: Collect
insurance policy payments but avoid paying claims. Airlines

insert terms and conditions that give them an out so they don't have to "give the seats away." They prefer an exchange of points for things other than flights, and they set expiration dates that cancel the points.

Avoid Painful Precedents

Continental Airlines balked when I tried to consummate a limited-time offer it had made on points for overseas flights. Each time I tried to get two first-class seats, as per the offer, seats were "not available." Reason: Airlines reserve the right to limit the number of available seats and impose blackout periods. In other words, promote the points but ration the seats. After several failed attempts to get what was promised, I got through to a Continental lawyer. I said that if Continental continued to pretend that seats were available when they weren't, I would buy two first-class seats and sue Continental for the cost because it was reneging on its offer. I added that if the judge or jury were Continental One Pass members, Continental would surely lose. She counseled: Pick a couple of flights, try again, and, if nothing is available, call her back. I did as directed. The seats were suddenly available.

Pretend Contracts

Corporations want us to believe that any piece of paper or plastic is a contract when they call it a contract. The paper may be a stub for a space in a parking garage or a seat for a live theater production, movie, or sporting event. It could be a plastic coat check token at a restaurant. An attendant may generate one at a parking garage before he drives off. All these supposed contracts teeter on shaky legal ground, even if the word *contract* appears on them.

Corporations want consumers to believe that these scraps of paper and plastic absolve the corporation of having to pay for its misdeeds. Their view is that if a problem occurs, holding up that little scrap with *contract* on it will ward off consumers the way holding up a cross will repel a vampire. A guerrilla consumerist sees it differently. The piece of paper is not a contract. It is just a piece of paper.

A contract is an agreement both parties knew about and agreed to *in advance.* A consumerist believes a contract is an agreement always subject to further negotiation: It does not let a corporation off the hook for a dent in the car that was not there when it was brought into the parking lot. Likewise, a consumerist believes a night at the opera is unsatisfactory if the ticket holder can't hear the opera. Unfortunately, Lincoln Center's David H. Koch Theater (previously known as the New York State Theatre) does not always take that into consideration.

We had a subscription for center-ring-orchestra seats. They were promoted as *premier orchestra,* a qualification to justify charging more for seats farther away from the stage than the ordinary orchestra seats. The performance by the New York City Opera was Sondheim's *A Little Night Music,* a musical designed for a much smaller Broadway-size theater. Jeremy Irons and other cast members became uncomfortable with the sound system. The director shut off the theater's sound system and gave the actors less-powerful body microphones. Talk about acoustic abuse. The farther audience members were from the stage, the less they could hear: The show's signature song, "Send in the Clowns," may as well have been performed as mime.

At intermission I tried to get a headset. Management stocked forty headsets. Management assumed that in a crowd of 2,755 listening without a general sound system, no more than 1.4% would request headsets. If demand exceeded supply, headset-deprived theatergoers would have to suffer silently, as long as they could be convinced that their sacrifice of audio reception enabled the show to go on.

The first response to my letter to the opera company's director of marketing did not disavow blame:

> *Our recent production of* A Little Night Music *was an eye-opening [sic] experience for us. Based on the many letters we received from our patrons, including yours, we have come to understand our use of body microphones was not sufficient amplification for this type of show.*[22]

Of course, the letter dodged financial accountability. No need for the company to establish a precedent for refunds, given its reluctance to put customers before performers. The letter continued like an Army telegram:

> *I regret to inform you that we are unable to issue a refund. You'll note that your tickets clearly state "Refunds are not available." This is City Opera policy, and is fairly standard for performing arts organizations.*

Like the parking lot industry, the theater business wants consumers to believe a ticket is a *contract.* On a ticket stub, that word is on shaky ground. Contract law assumes that contracts are read before they're signed. And there was a contract. The New York City Opera breached its obligation to provide the usual and traditional sound for paying customers. And note the industry's "fairly standard" defense, the last resort of naughty corporations.

I prepared my encore, reaching a marketing fellow named Brian Chapman who promised a refund. I don't know whether that led to his dismissal or he found a better job, but he disappeared from the New York City Opera's staff after he promised me a refund. I learned that when I brought up his unfulfilled promise when I received the City Opera's subscription renewal offer. My conditions for renewal depended on the company keeping Mr. Chapman's promise—and a pledge that the sound system would be turned on for future performances of musical comedies.

The company offered me two complimentary best-of-the-best ring seats for any future performance in the next season. We saw (and heard) *Carmen*. Two front-row ring seats in 2003 cost $190. The city opera would not promise to keep the system on, so we did not renew our subscription.

Magic Words

The words *ALL SALES FINAL—NO RETURNS OR CREDIT* on sales invoices are the last refuge of rogue corporations. What if a consumerist later finds hidden flaws, especially in products priced as top-quality garments? As consumerists, we reserve the right to determine when words matter and when they don't. Such as when I bought a Barbara Bui suit for my wife in 1996.

Barbara Bui is a famous name in high-priced women's clothing. Labels like hers lift the retail markup to nosebleed heights. As luck would have it, just as my wife and I entered the Barbara Bui room on Bergdorf Goodman's fabled fourth floor, every item was reduced by 80%. It was a dramatic moment when the luxury apparel industry's controlled pricing system worked in our favor.

My wife chose a two-piece Bui suit made from a woolen fabric, with fleecy, three-dimensional feathery lapels. The price was reduced from $1,850 to $370.

After ten months and several glorious outings, Bui's three-dimensional lapels went two-dimensional on my wife, due to a slow-stage molting that induced feathery pieces to fly off as if in search of the birds from whence they came. The suit was aging before its time. We shipped the Bui back to Bergdorf's, requesting an explanation of the quality problems and a replacement. A month passed without response.

My call to Customer Service went to a Ms. Dooley, the new fourth-floor manager. She researched the Bui return status and confirmed that Bergdorf Goodman had received the suit, but could not locate it. She promised to look into it, but as a precaution asked how much we paid for it.

Retailers like to think that what a customer paid for an item is not as significant as what it's actually worth. Imaginative consumerists remind retailers that the opposite is true. Phrases like *current value* and *replacement cost* come in handy during confrontations like these. Ms. Dooley was obviously fishing for a number in case BG had to compensate me for losing the suit.

Consider this: Expensive clothes are displayed as if they were works of art. Therefore, owning a Bui is like owning a Picasso, right? If the Museum of Modern Art lost a Picasso, would the value decrease from the original purchase price? My answer to Ms. Dooley: "I think it sold for around $1,800." That was true. That had been its stated value a few minutes before we bought it.

Ms. Dooley abandoned the search and admitted that BG had lost the suit. There was another problem. BG had stopped doing business with Barbara Bui, so there was no way for BG to replace it. Ms. Dooley apologized and hoped I had found a record of the purchase. Like a politician under oath, I said I "could not recall" because to do so would not have been in my interest. She made an offer: $1,250 credit. We took it. I paid $370 for an $880 increase in purchasing power.

THE MBA MIND-SET

There is much to be learned from understanding the MBA mind-set. A well-educated, smart MBA is a valuable asset that can engineer language and change management structure, and manage the market to get outcomes that advance the fortunes of a corporation without taking too many casualties.

If you want to know how an MBA's mind works, invite one to your home and give him/her a tour of where you live and who lives with you. You see your furniture in terms of comfort and convenience. An MBA sees them as future opportunities to sell replacement upholstery, rollers, and cushions.

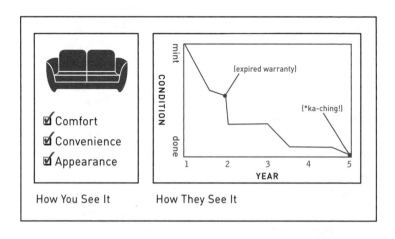

☑ Comfort
☑ Convenience
☑ Appearance

CONDITION — mint ... done

YEAR — 1 2 3 4 5

(expired warranty)

(*ka-ching!)

How You See It   How They See It

You see your family as people. The MBA sees them as representative samples of market segments represented by age, income and buying patterns. Take your children for example: They are the flesh and blood on whom you are determined to eternally bestow your unconditional love (even when they jump up and down on the brand-new living room furniture, thereby hastening the arrival of the moment when you will have to replace it). But the marketing team at McDonald's sees your children as a way to deliver you into their line-up for the latest Happy Meal deal, which is why the restaurant's color scheme and advertising campaigns are so relentlessly youth-oriented. Thanks, Mom and Dad—we're one of the billions served!

How You See Your Kids   How They See Your Kids

You saw the 2008 financial crisis as a recession. An MBA sees it as "self-correction." If you see an unemployment rate at 10%, the MBA sees it as 90% employed and ready to buy something.

The MBA is locked into a belief system that explains why what seems bad is actually good because it flows from the force known as the Market. Further, that the Market is shaped by an awesome and irresistible force known as "the invisible hand." First used by economist Adam Smith in *The Wealth of Nations* to describe a principle of foreign versus domestic trade, the invisible hand has become a metaphor for the self-correcting process that leads only to good things, and whose fingerprints therefore never appear on any bad things. In other words, it is a "natural" self-correction that works best when unhampered by regulators and legislators.

The MBA believes the Market works best when left to its own devices. The MBA believes every negative principle at work can be artfully explained in a PowerPoint presentation with six-color pie charts. At their most dangerous to us, an MBA literally believes that whatever his/her corporation does can be explained in ways that do minimal damage and maximum good to the corporation. Fellow consumerists, beware of true believers with MBA degrees. (See page 175.)

The Great Transference

The MBA knows the perils of technology: The more complex the technology, the greater the likelihood of operational failure. Failure is expensive, whether involving a product under development or after the sale. Stopping production to fix a defect is costly and wreaks havoc on delivery schedules. Quality and service costs erode profits. The MBA's solution is to transfer liability anywhere outside the company. But how to pull off the transfer without crowds gathering to protest and throw things at corporate headquarters? It requires management finesse. The bigger the corporation, the less time management can spare for consumer complaints. Many consumers fantasize about trying to reach The Man (or The Woman) in charge of

The Corporation. Not bloody likely. And if a corporation does put out the friendly face of corporate leadership, you'd better believe the corporation is not doing it to show it cares. Never expect to get the address where the bigwigs work. But that shouldn't stop the consumerist from trying to reach those in the corner office with the panoramic views. Send letters, e-mails—anything that begs for a response. Your local reference librarian can be an ally in the fight. Librarians can find the corporate HQ in a flash by accessing all sorts of library-based databases. Once you start a chain of communication, you open the path to compensation. What titan of industry ever wants to be perceived as The Man who ignores the cries of the Little People?

Blame the Victim

This is corporate tactic worth revisiting because it's one of the most common—and evil. Companies try to convert a complaint into an "it's your fault" issue. If you accept that, the grievance ends there. So—and I want to stress this—*never* accept blame, even if part of a problem started with something you did, like waiting too long for a melon to ripen or ironing a no-iron fabric. Customer Service might tell you the problem could have been avoided had you read the manual, been more careful, or simply lowered your expectations. You bought it. You own it.

Baloney. Think of it this way: You paid for it. The service person you are speaking with gets paid to get rid of people like you.

BP would have blamed its 2010 oil spill on Nostradamus if it could have. MBAs also get a dose of consumer psychology for their $80,000 tuition. They know you might cave if they lay on the blame hard enough. Hold your ground.

Send Consumers to Do-It-Yourself Non-Solutions

Nobody on top loves a hotshot executive more than when he can rig the system to funnel complaints through a maze of websites and voice-sensitive phone systems. Let the masses bitch to a page of FAQs. That'll take care of most of 'em.

Reduce Consumers to a Few Consumerists

The enemy is aware that a few consumers are smart enough to hang in there until comp is offered. The enemy aims to derail the majority and to tolerate—and if need be, pay off the persistent.

Onward, comrades! You are ready for Chapter 8.

CHAPTER 8

TOOLS AND WEAPONS FOR CONSUMERISTS

CONFIDENTIAL: For Consumerist Eyes Only

This chapter contains confidential information of a sensitive nature. If it falls into enemy hands, consumerists will be put at unnecessary risk. Only consumerists with High-Level Security Clearance are permitted to read beyond this point.

PREPAREDNESS

We are at war. War will astonish you.

You decide, soldier: When you have grown old and are looking back on your life, do you want to tell your grandchildren that you were abused by a corporation and you just let it happen? Or do you want to tell them that whenever a corporation abused you, you fought back and made the bastards pay? We shall shock and awe the enemy. If that doesn't work, we'll get a full refund.

THE CHOICE IS YOURS

Types of Compensation

Compensation varies from cash to credits to frequent-flier points to a papaya FedExed to me after I complained about a papaya being too green. Compensation types are not equal. These are, in order of their worth: *cash, cash equivalents* (such as charge cancellations or credits), *replacement* products worth more or the same as whatever product failed to please you, *limited credits* for use only with the offending corporation, *coupons for free products, coupons for sums of money* to reduce the cost of a product you want, *points* (as in frequent-flier points, worth between $.01 to $.05 each in buying power), and *free extensions of contracts* (like subscriptions for cable or magazines). Always try for a combination of comps.

Upgrades at no charge are welcome. Assignment of true dollar value is subject to one's imagination.

See Appendix B's Compensation Evaluation Form.

Credit Cards

Credit cards are better for consumerist purposes than debit cards. Credit cards have a period of time between purchase and payment during which you can dispute a charge before it is technically paid. Debit cards allow the enemy to have your money before the purchase is bagged and in your hands. For smaller amounts, challenges by cardholders with good credit usually result in a credit. For larger sums, the banks push the corporation to answer the complaint. You are the customer the bank wants to keep.

I recommend having at least two credit card accounts from two different banks. If there should be a dispute with one of the banks, having a second card gives you a credible fallback option when you threaten to cancel the other card.

Checking Accounts

As with credit cards, have two different checking accounts, unless they come with monthly service charges. Always have a backup account. Banks are in stiff competition with each other for your business.

Documentation

A consumerist must be ready to document a purchase—to use with a complaint letter—or show an implied guarantee in a promotional promise. Not having documentation is like wearing bedroom slippers instead of combat boots. Start the battle fully documented. You need three basic forms:

Sales receipts for valuable items: These are for insurance as well. Retain them for the life of the product or service.

Monthly credit card charge summaries: Abuses can emerge long after a purchase. Either keep monthly statements or be certain that they are available online at no charge.

Sales receipts from supermarkets: Needed for regular returns of foods not as fresh as promised or not as sweet as promised. Eat plenty of fresh vegetables and fruit—and return portions as needed. Remember: You establish whether the stuff made the grade, not them.

Scam Sensitivity

Scams have increased due to lack of regulation of the Internet, the growth globalization, and a deficiency of enforcement of existing regulation. You are on your own. Crafty scammers can trick the savviest consumerist. The Federal Trade Commission issues regulations but has little interest in enforcement on behalf of consumers.

Do not trust any unsolicited call, no matter how familiar the product or service sounds or how friendly the caller is. If there is a two- or three-second pause between picking up the call and connection to an operator, a scam may be under way via an automated dialing system by crooks located in venues that make it hard or impossible for you to do much to them.

FIRST-STRIKE DELIVERY SYSTEMS (FSDS) FOR CONSUMERISTS

Internet
Establish your beachhead on the Internet. Most corporations have websites with a contact pathway. Starting a complaint via e-mail is cost-efficient and may be the sole action needed. Food production corporations will send coupons worth more than the product you attack, particularly when you include the barcode number and expiration date in the complaint.

I bought a can of Del Monte canned string beans (about $2). Usually they are perfect. The can contained one bean that had the equivalent of age spots. Another bean still had the stem attached. I sent a quick e-mail to Del Monte via its website. Back came four coupons: Three were for $1.95 each for any Del Monte canned product, one for 50 cents off a "ketchup product." Total $6.35. A net of $4.35 from a $2 purchase we ate, minus one bean and a stem. Total elapsed time: ten minutes. That's $30 an hour, the rate for someone making $60,000 a year.

Toll-Free Phone Numbers
If Customer Service answers promptly and intelligently, that's good for the customer who wants answers but bad for the consumerist who wants compensation. If the corporations dodge and weave, play music you do not enjoy, or claim heavy call volume, bingo! You have hit a good target. But it will require

attention and time. Stay with it. The enemy has selected music previously tested on focus groups to determine how long it will take to make consumers hang up. The same tactic may be in play when callers are put on silent **terminal hold**. That's waiting to the sound of your breathing—without Musak.

Ordinary Mail

A letter has more impact now than when it was the only means for consumers to air grievances. A letter addressed to an officer of the corporation, with copies of receipts or quotations from promotions, usually gets attention—unless you send it to Whole Foods or AT&T. Corporations are increasingly uncertain as to how to handle a *letter*. If your first letter is not answered within ten days, send a copy and suggest that you might file a complaint with an Internet blog (see Resources section) or the Better Business Bureau or a columnist who writes about consumer issues. The idea is not to exercise any of those options—unless a lot of money is at issue—but to remind a corporation that it might be better to deal with you than the watchdogs you might invite in.

MEANS TO YOUR ENDS

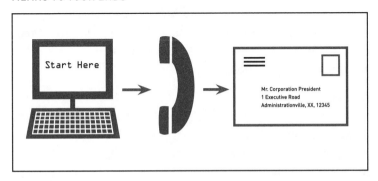

Start Here

Mr. Corporation President
1 Executive Road
Administrationville, XX, 12345

Spectacular Returns

Special circumstances require special attention. When I was young and naive, I bought a set of tires while driving cross-country. A sharp-eyed Phillips 66 gas station attendant on I-80 convinced me that I should trade in my tires right now before I crossed the red-hot desert in Utah on my way to California. I fell for it. I paid with a Phillips 66 credit card. A month later in California I decided to replace the spare. The tire dealer said the tires I bought were bigger than recommended. He could not guarantee the fifth tire of the same size as the new four.

We made a deal. I bought five tires, provided he box the four oversized tires so I could ship them back to Phillips 66 headquarters in the Midwest. Off they went, COD. Phillips 66 issued a complete credit. (The five tires cost less than the oversized four.)

I once returned a Christmas tree. The needles fell off too soon. I was given a bigger and better one.

Want to make a point? Make a creative return.

WEAPONS OF MANAGEMENT DESTRUCTION (WMD)

Just as the enemy does not seek to destroy us, we do not seek to destroy the enemy. (Like I said, war can be astonishing.) The enemy wishes to keep selling us things in the future and avoid confrontations over purchases in the past. We seek compensation for abuses past and those to come.

Threat Credibility

A credible threat may be enough to win suitable comp. However, never make a threat that you are unprepared to implement. Corporations hear and read threats all day long, most of which are empty and dyspeptic. Corporations will not be intimidated by a threat to throw a brick through one of their windows. They welcome an excuse to disconnect or call the cops because, either way, they change the subject and make the consumer look bad.

Corporations pay attention to unusual threats and complaints, however. May I suggest wrapping a brick in velvet and sending it to a CEO with the note, "It is tempting to throw this at you, but I prefer a nonviolent approach." Or you could write, "Like your organization, I also have policies: I do not pay Late Fees or Early Termination Charges or the cost of sending defective products back."

The best threats convey the problem and your real threat, but hold out the possibility of a peaceful resolution:

- If you cannot fix this problem, I'll dispute the charge with the credit card company and we'll see whom the bank believes.
- I may have to take this to Small Claims Court. You'd better hope the judge has not done business with your company.
- You are wasting my time by not having the answer to my question. I will expect something for my time and your lack of knowledge. Or I will find someone else.

In war, peaceful solutions aren't reached through diplomacy.

Code Words

Live operators who take toll-free calls have screens in front of them with word prompts that tell them what to say or where to send a caller. Likewise, you should use words like *manager, executive level, refund, disputed charge, return,* or *corporate headquarters.*

I was going nowhere with a Comcast complaint until I used the word *management.* Later a Comcast employee told me that unless I used that word, the manager who authorized credits had instructed people not to send him any calls. In that instance, I received about $60 in monthly credits. AT&T has an *executive level resolution* prompt used for tough-minded consumerists—although if corporate execs read this page, AT&T may change the name. Citibank has an *Office of the President*.

BREAK THEIR CODES

Tough Questions for Consumerists to Ponder

What is your time worth? The corporation ought to thank you for bringing matters to its attention. You are pointing out a problem a caring corporation should pay you for: You deserve an unsolicited consulting fee for offering to help a corporation improve what it does. They pay consultants, don't they?

The time needed depends on a corporation's Dissatisfaction Management Plan. If you're gobbling up minutes trying to connect with a live human being, the corporation owes you something for your time.

Who the hell wrote those website FAQs? Does anyone update anything? FAQs have been written by experts who specialize in asking questions that prevent consumers from learning anything about serious problems with a product or service. Corporations do not wish to spend money on websites to service what you already bought. Instead, they use websites to sell you something you haven't thought of buying, but might. In addition, corporate websites are out of sync with what's happening in the here and now.

Continental Airlines (now merged with United) canceled a flight we were to take the next day because of expected bad weather. That was the right thing to do. But Continental continued to sell tickets for that flight although already canceled. Wrong thing to do. It also didn't build much confidence in its website's ability to stay up-to-date and be a one-stop shop. I received 10,000 extra frequent-flier miles as compensation. Were there any collateral costs? Do not get stuck on the "purchase price platform"—unless it works to your advantage. When calculating how much a defective item or service has already cost, a consumerist considers collateral costs like service fees, annual memberships, monthly charges, any account termination charge, any account transfer fee, any ticket service fee, and fulfillment. Then round up.

How irritated are you? Corporations often pay an "inconvenience fee" to an upset consumer, especially when a corporation already has heard from other customers with the same problem. Such payments are seldom volunteered. To get them, dramatize your irritation. Try the *controlled fury* tactic: "Look, I know you didn't make this piece of junk, that you're just doing your job. But I am mad as hell that I even have to make this damn call—not to mention all the time I have lost listening to the same ads on your recorded message. By the way, I did not like the music that was playing." Share your pain. People new to consumerism may find it hard to quantify anger. Practice makes perfect. If you still are hesitant, have another look at the worth of your time. It's a nonrenewable resource. (Still no anger? Seek counseling.)

Disputed Charges

Disputed is a hot-button word because of its legal implications. It suggests that there are grounds for questioning the legitimacy of a charge that appears on your card. Do not use it casually. Have the hard evidence to justify the dispute. Put the burden on the corporation to justify the charge.

For example, when New York Presbyterian Hospital and Blue Cross each sent letters telling me that Blue Cross did not cover a $1,645 routine, annual lab test for my wife, I was not surprised. We do not have, nor ever did have, Blue Cross coverage. The surprise was the size of the bill, compared to charges for a similar test in the past—as in $1,500 more.

The hospital billing office's non-response to calls ended when the word *dispute* was joined to the phrase *no payment for anything* until New York Presbyterian documented the charge. Yet the hospital kept on billing. Here are excerpts from my letter to its CEO. I was venting and panning for payoff at the same time.

> *WE KNOW BEST. It took hours to get people at the hospital and Blue Cross to offer any explanation or correction. At work was a "We know best" attitude that either puts most patients off or covers up errors leading to overpayment that can go forever undetected by NY-P.* The lack of NY-P checkpoints to protect consumers from errors is an indication that you need better management. Evidently it will only come after regulation and investigation. *That*

is why a copy of this letter is being sent to [then Attorney General] Andrew Cuomo's office. Summary:

PATIENT DIY. In October I was told by NY-P that had I paid the $1,645 bill, the overcharge would have never been detected by NY-P. That puts patients into Do-It-Yourself mode, an approach better suited to Walmart than NY-P.

THE DOCTOR DID IT. NY-P's first line of defense in October was that [the doctor's] office submitted inept paperwork that set this thing in motion. Wrong.

MIXUP. Next NY-P admitted its error. NY-P explained the root cause was a "mix-up" with a patient whose last name and records were similar to my wife's data. If so, it is a statistical coincidence worthy of the New England Journal of Medicine: *Similar last and first names, similar tests, similar last four Social Security digits, and same doctor? In your mind, what does* mix-up *stand for?*

NEVER FIXED. In my call last week, the billing person said it was a processing error. She was surprised that the processing error is not yet fixed. I think I can see what she means: The latest statement NY-P sent is incomprehensible: BLUE CROSS appears five times in line items. The most useless line is BLUE CROSS TRANSFER TO BLUE CROSS. What? BC is transferring a cost to BC that BC does not cover? (Wait a minute: Is BC a government agency?) Do you think this document is patient-friendly? Has it been tried out on focus groups? (Or on the NY-P Board of Directors?) If this is happening to us, it is happening to other people less inclined or prepared to question a bill like this. NY-P's resistance to explain or correct the error demonstrates nonchalant . . . negligence.

The CEO looked into it. He quickly found it was a full-blown error—and called to apologize. We owed about $145, which he canceled, together with the $1,500 overcharge.

Disputed "Credit Reports"

Your refusal to pay a disputed charge may stimulate a threat to report you to a credit rating agency. If your nonpayment is on solid ground, write *DISPUTED* on the threatening letter and briefly summarize past communications with statements like these: "This matter has been discussed, and I have explained why I am disputing this charge. Be sure to tell the agency that I disputed the charge and tell them why."

The threats are often phony. A corporate department that pretends to be a collection or rating agency might be sending the threats. Call their bluff by inviting them to sue and reminding them that the matter is in a dispute the corporation has chosen to ignore.

Deadlines

Establish a deadline for a corporation to act. My favorites are either ten or thirty calendar days. Either is reasonable and provides the foundation for a case. Often I'll write, "If I have not heard from you by oo/oo/oooo, I will consider the matter closed." This is, of course, nonsense. Nevertheless, it reminds the enemy that they will be encountering a veteran with whom they would be wise to settle.

Potential Allies

Consumer-friendly websites are out there—and changing at a fast clip. See Appendix C for a list of websites that may be helpful, but keep in mind that an hour after this book is printed, changes could have occurred. Sites can go stale or disappear in a hurry. Gadflies in newspapers and on TV can also be of help. Consumer mistreatment builds readership and ratings. Just don't exaggerate as you describe your grievance. If you get caught embellishing, you might undermine your entire argument.

Intelligence goes both ways, of course. Counter consumerism is growing at larger corporations. Counter-consumerist agents scour the Internet for bad publicity generated by product and service defects written about in blogs—like my **www.consumeristmanifesto.net.** Their job is to discredit consumerists. They are clever, but they lack one thing: a just cause. They are the running dogs of enemy corporations. You can beat them almost every time.

Small Claims Court

Think hard before you resort to Small Claims Court to wring compensation out of a corporation. The paperwork consumes time. The permissible claims do not allow for "pain and suffering" or punitive damages. The legal procedures give an advantage to corporations, especially if a consumer's residence is not in the same county, state, or even country as the corporate headquarters.

But if a consumer can show legitimate, measurable costs caused by what a corporation did or did not do, a corporation may shy away from the court showdown or avoid it altogether. When you file a claim, the corporation must show up or risk the likelihood that the judge will "find" for the consumer in the corporation's absence. Showing up is expensive for both sides—but more so for a corporation. The corporation will coldly calculate the credibility of the consumer's gripe and lawyer up, if need be. However, a valid threat to take the matter to

Small Claims may move the matter forward out of court. This missive spells out ugly consequences for any firm considering taking a consumerist up on the judicial route:

> OK. This is where we are. I am going to file for damages in Small Claims Court. I'll describe the problem and your lack of response to the judge. You or your corporate lawyer can tell the judge your side. If I were you, I would hope the judge has not bought this product from you guys. If you really think I am a nutcase, invite the press in.

Before you commit to Small Claims, do your homework. Bone up on the rules and procedures of the Small Claims Court in the municipality where the business is located. Lots of people threaten to go to Small Claims Court. Managers have heard that sort of threat before. Do not threaten unless you are willing to go forward.

Small Claims can also bite you back. In 2005, I was billed about $1,000 for a special set of x-rays ordered by a major hospital. The films were done by a facility recommended by the hospital. The facility did not realize it did not have the proper equipment, until the hospital said so hours after receipt of the films. The facility asked that a sister facility do the x-rays again with different equipment in a different location. That meant an extra day of time and trouble to get it done the way it should have been done. I refused to pay the bill.

After a year of polite company requests for payment, answered each time by my refusal, the facility turned it over to its lawyer. We talked. He did to me what I have done to corporations: made a credible threat to go to small claims court. He was not bluffing. A day before the trial, I asked for a delay, which small claims courts almost automatically grant. That angered the lawyer because he had to reschedule himself and the witness from one of the facilities—an expense not recoverable in the Small Claims system. He recognized the tactic for what it was. It is disruptive to have to reschedule at the last minute. When a new date was set, I got another delay. The lawyer called to have an amiable phone chat. He proposed a settlement less than 33% of the original bill. I accepted because it turned out the films worked well enough. Big corporations do not like Small Claims Courts because they give the little guy a place to tell his story—and, no matter what the outcome, the corporation loses.

Last Resort: The BBB

The Better Business Bureau walks a tightrope. The name suggests it is an agency set up to protect consumers. Not exactly: Corporations pay dues to the BBB as a way of extricating themselves from problems with consumers. The dues are based on the size of the corporation. As with any large organization, the biggest gorillas in the room are given the most room to maneuver. Corporations do not shell out annual fees to not-for-profits without malice aforethought.

The BBB offers to arbitrate and mediate disputes between consumers and corporations. It keeps files on disputes, which can be accessed by consumers. The BBB's problem is that it rates a company's standing by how few complaints the company generates, rather than verifying the company's behavior for itself.

CORPORATE DEFENSE SYSTEMS (CDS)

Our Consumerist Intelligence Unit has analyzed the current trends gleaned from skirmishes with large corporate defense systems. Generally speaking, corporations can deploy many strategies to reduce complaints to the lowest acceptable number.

The greater the corporate investment in promotional activities, the more sophisticated the deployment of defense tactics.

MANEUVERING IN A CDS

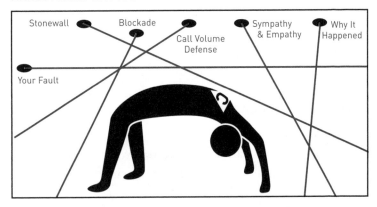

The list below starts with the weakest and cheapest CDS choices and moves up as customers get tougher to dismiss. Callouts in italics indicate corporations that practice the specified tactic.

Stonewall: Do not take calls, answer letters, or respond to e-mails. *Whole Foods*

Blockade: Dig electronic dead-ends to send consumers into passageways that lead nowhere or back to where they started. *Hewlett-Packard*

Call Volume Defense: Reduce the number of operators, select the least qualified to answer, and offer the recorded message, "Due to unexpected heavy volume, we cannot answer your call at this time." *AT&T*

Sympathy & Empathy: Outsource calls to Bangalore, India, and train people to apologize and disconnect. *Covad Communications*

Why It Happened: Use an explanation like "a mix-up" to explain away what happened, as if a knucklehead blunder is exempt from consumer action. *New York Presbyterian Hospital Billing Services*

Usual and Standard Industry Practice (USIP): Just say this is the way all corporations have always operated in our industry, so it's OK. *insurance industry, theater industry, agriculture industry, and telecom-industrial complex*

Your Fault: You brought it on yourself. *General Motors, several corporate healthcare companies*

Another Corporation's Fault: The fault-free argument, asserting that "We didn't do it," so it's not our responsibility. *Comcast* Once you penetrate their defenses, they put the Negotiated Settlement or Preplanned Payment on the table.

RESULTS MEASUREMENT

Worth of Time Revisited

Seasoned consumerists know how to calculate the worth of their time. The system: If you have a job that pays you at an hourly rate, you have a *starting number*. If not, use your annual salary. If you're unemployed or retired, use your last good year. For every $1,000 of annual salary, use $1.00/hour, based on a 40-hour week for 50 weeks, or 2,000 work hours in a year. If none fit your circumstances, use the minimum wage in your state.

Annual Wages	Worth Formula
$20,000	20 x 1 = $20/hour
$50,000	50 x 1 = $50/hour
$75,000	75 x 1 = $75/hour

Consider using the Consultants Doubling Principle, a favorite of consultants for determining a fee to charge corporations. Or simply come up with a base fee and double it. The higher the fee, the more valuable the consultant appears to be.

Think of your complaint as useful information for a corporation. You're providing insights that a consultant would. But that doesn't mean the corporation is smart enough to pay attention. You are giving customer feedback and the corporate honchos ought to be grateful enough to pay you for it. They amply compensate consultants, so they should pay you.

Evidence of Results

It comes down to your bottom line: What has being an active consumerist done for your bottom line?

WHERE THINGS ARE HEADED

In the end, we consumerists will be more on our own than ever before.

Without much fanfare or public notice, we have moved from being a *nation state* to becoming a *market state*.[23] This was not a corporate idea. There was no conspiracy. It is just how things are working out. A few manufacturers trump the many citizens.

Legislation for serious consumer protection is outgunned by well-financed forces that unleash the authorize-but-don't-allocate chimera: An agency or office is authorized to establish consumer protection for a product, but the resources needed are not allocated to do the job. Thus, a politician can establish a record that he shows concern for consumer protection and spending restraint, but the latter precludes the former.

Staffing of agencies is a tool to block enforcement of rules that protect consumers. Agency leadership can be blocked by one senator, who can nix a high-level appointment based only on the argument, "Not that one." The privilege is used to eliminate candidates that an important industry or constituent sees as a threat. When Elizabeth Warren, a scholar credited with the idea of the Consumer Financial Protection Bureau, was the Obama administration's top choice to head the bureau, the financial services industry went into high alert. No surprise, given that the new agency said its mission was to "prevent abusive, deceptive, and fraudulent terms for mortgages, credit cards, payday loans, and a vast array of other financial products." The financial services forces got part of what they wanted: President Obama quietly nominated someone else (and they will try to shove that person out as well). No outrage, no comment from the president.

Consumers are not an organized force.

Joe Nocera, the *New York Times* business columnist, interviewed Warren after the financial services folks won the battle. He commented on "the disparity between what she's actually done [in setting up the CFPB] versus the Republican demonization of her: It is true . . . she raised hell "about the tricks and traps" too often used by the financial services industry to gouge its customers . . . but she mostly stressed the importance of clear disclosure and easy-to-read contracts."[24]

A consumerist movement, even one grounded in the cause of right, inevitably becomes more corporate as it grows: A dedicated staff, a mission statement, a logo, fund-raising, e-blasts, promotional campaigns, offices, a **human resources department**, and lobbyists all become part of the deal. Such a movement would be "the full catastrophe," to quote Zorba the Greek. Consumerist warfare, at least the kind I engage in for profit and giggles, is best waged by small, often one-man or one-woman, armies.

WHAT CONSUMERISTS DON'T NEED

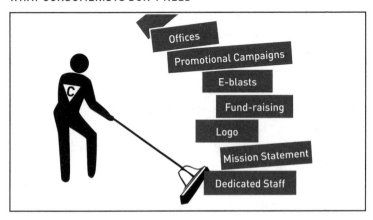

CONSUMERIST ACTION BEATS CLASS ACTION

Our plight is exemplified by how class action suits are managed. The real winners are attorneys who specialize in these suits. They get fees or percentages of the take—and they get them first. The "class" in a class action suit has become the elite. Procedural gobbledygook now prevents a majority of stockholders or stakeholders from filing a claim as part of the "class," thereby preserving settlement dollars for the few with the largest dollar holdings. Being abused does not count unless you are also large. So, in the end, class action is mostly for show, right along with the Better Business Bureau and Small Claims Court.

The one chink in the armor of corporations is that they have not yet been able to annihilate the competition. They can acquire many competitors, weaken some, but they cannot eliminate all of them. They can abuse us, and rig regulators and regulations, but enough competition exists in nearly every industry for us to make most corporations eventually listen and pay for their abuses. They will deal with us if we creatively persist and stick to our priorities, such as going after the worst offenders with the deepest pockets. With their morality as our guide, we shall continue to support the status quo and go after the cash.

TWO FOOTNOTES TO TWO GREAT MISFORTUNES
Tarnished Goldman[25]

In fairness to Goldman Sachs CEO Lloyd Blankfein, he may actually believe what he said after all of us bailed out the financial services industry in 2009: that Goldman Sachs and the other masters of finance were just innocent bystanders in the near-meltdown of the economy. Goldman Sachs was nothing more than a middleman between buyers and sellers, providing revenues for companies that create jobs. "I am doing God's work," Lloyd said. Imagine that: The invisible hand of free market forces teamed up with a deity thrown in as a back-up. He follows in the tradition of royalty who believed in the divine right of kings. But his deity defense failed. Goldman settled the matter by paying a $550 million fine for securities fraud.

Leaky Defense

The BP oil spill of 2010 is further evidence of an emerging market state. BP was regulated by the Minerals Management Service (MMS), a government agency that set new records for non-enforcement of regulations by regulators. When it came to enforcing safety standards, BP regulated the MMS. BP's contradictory statements in the early days of the disaster—plus its harsh treatment of its own employees—reflected the arrogance of corporate power that can shrug off a couple of billion dollars in reparations and prepare for the next drilling. BP made disparaging remarks about the "little people" near the Gulf of Mexico who dared to criticize BP. Next came a disinformation campaign about how the oil was almost all cleaned up. It said it would pay the costs and stay as long as it takes, all of which BP will define as it goes along. Eventually, BP set up a $20 billion reparations fund for individuals and businesses affected—with the caveat that anyone who receives compensation from the fund cannot sue. (As of April 2011, $3.6 billion has been paid out, according to the *New York Times*.)

Why does any of this matter in a book for consumerists? Goldman Sachs and BP filed for tax deductions as part of their stupendous settlements. BP claimed a $10 billion credit for the $32 billion in losses it claims to have sustained as a result of its own recklessness and stupidity. That's a third of the damage that will not go into our federal coffers and a third off their bill. It's the collateral taxpayer cost of *punitive damages*. *Punitive* sounds good, especially when corporations are dangerously negligent. Yet punitive damages are tax-deductible as a business expense against earnings. This loophole somehow got into the corporate tax laws, possibly as another instance of God's work. If you or I had to pay punitive damages for something we did wrong, we could not deduct the charges to reduce our taxes. Goldman eventually decided not to pursue a $187 million credit for its payout. The outrage that would have followed would have been bad for its image.

PART 3

RESOURCES

When I chat with consumers, it always strikes me as odd that they do not add the value of their time that was needed to implement a complaint about an abuse in their demand for compensation. It's as if their time is not part of the problem created by that abuse. What's more, the time needed is amplified by the enemy's use of delaying tactics, transfer-of-blame games, and stonewalling in order to wear out consumers who seek just communication regarding demands for compensation. This in itself is an abuse.

Part of being a successful consumerist is the recognition that since time is a non-renewable resource, it is precious and valuable. (And can be measured.) Once a consumer catches on that the amount of time needed to build and deliver a complaint should be included in the compensation as billable minutes or hours, that consumer becomes a *consumerist*.

Use the resources provided here as tools to help you quantify and qualify your time and the comp you deserve. This section will help you better understand the abuses you've suffered and organize them in a way that will be useful when you are seeking proper comp, thus cutting down the time and energy you exhaust in your pursuit of justice.

CORP-SPEAK GLOSSARY

The meaning of words can be troublesome. Businesses revise old words and phrases to legitimize their wrongdoing. For instance, *orchestra* is about location when it describes a seat—usually on the same floor as the stage—with an implication of having a premium view. But suppose the orchestra seat somehow compromises sight or sound? Like when the angle prevents you from seeing the action on the sides of the stage? Or when a pillar blocks your view, like a foul pole at a baseball stadium? *Partial view*—vaguely defined—to the rescue.

As I touched on earlier, corporate language experts create new words and phrases that combine explanation with obfuscation. The corporate world rivals the military in the expansion of acronyms and abbreviations. Acronyms are preferred because they are easier to remember and say: Corporations will hire an ASS (Acronym Spelling Specialist) to review corporate communications for acronym opportunities.

Note: The red entries below are original—unless unconsciously pilfered by me. If I have mistakenly "borrowed" when I thought I created, the following USIP applies: That's what writers do.

Abuse Cluster. A situation with multiple abuses, discovered either immediately upon impact or later during evaluation for compensation.

Advertar. A visual ad, created by hidden software algorithms, tailored for and aimed at one consumer. Eli Pariser created this word in *The Filter Bubble*. (See Further Reading.)

Algorithm. Mathematical formula that produces an impressive number for use during a PowerPoint presentation. Practical use unknown.

AQ. *Assurance of Quality.* Step(s) taken to assure that quality will have minimal repercussions on the corporate bottom line. See *QC*.

Bailout. Consumer rescue of **banksters** drowning in the Sea of Red Ink.

Bankster. Word reintroduced during the Great Recession of 2008. Merger of *banker* and *gangster*. (Used by radio evangelist Father Charles Coughlin in the 1930s to attack FDR, communists, and Jews who, according to him, were part of the evil empire.)

Benefits. From the corporate perspective: *What can the consumer do to benefit us? Which benefits can be promised without being delivered?* From the consumer's perspective: *Where are the benefits I thought I bought?*

Best Practices. Legal phrase that allows a corporation to get away with "worst practices." Inserted in new product offerings (**NPOs**), consumer contracts, warranties, and summaries to juries by corporate defense lawyers. (See also *Mice Type*.)

Billing Cycle. Time period shrunk to minimize the number of days between when a bill is sent and when it must be paid to maximize application of automatic late charges and interest payments.

BIMP. *Business Management Professional.* Rhymes with another professional who will do anything to sell his streetwalking merchandise.

Boutique Music. Music composed to reduce consumer resistance. Variations calibrated to demographic groups. Chirpy and optimistic (ages 18–35), uplifting and reassuring (36–64), and pleasant but louder (senior citizens). See *Hold Music*.

Bribes. Usually defined as the cash incentives corporations use to get unhappy regulators off their backs. Broadly defined, includes dinners, executive seats at theaters, and professional sports events. Tax-deductible when transmogrified into business expenses. (See *Rigging*.)

Bundle or Bundling. Required purchase of a product of no value to acquire a product of value because the latter is only available when "bundled" with the former. Examples: 1. Grade B movie shown with a Grade A in a double feature. 2. Cable industry practice, as opposed to à la carte channel selection and pricing.

Business Model. For public consumption: A summary of how a corporation organizes its business to reach its defined market segments. For company eyes only: The public model with footnotes on how to manipulate consumers and tax filings to maximize profits.

CAPPS. *Capping in Advance of Penalty Payment Steps.* Strategy by which corporations limit their liability in advance to protect against lawsuits for negligence.

Captive Agency. A federal or state regulatory agency that transfers allegiance to an industry, such as those involved in oil and shale exploration.

CDQs. *Consumer-Designed Questions* to inject a greater sense of reality into corporate FAQs. Examples of questions we might be frequently asking:

- If my call is so important, why does it take so long to be answered?
- May I speak with a corporate manager who thinks my call is "very important"?
- Where on your website is the answer you said would be there?
- Why does no one in Customer Service know your corporate address?

Celebrification. Utilization of an instantly recognizable celebrity who praises a not-yet-seen product to stimulate advance sales.

Comp. Compensation received by consumerists in the form of cash, credits, coupons, useful replacements, discounts, and reduced charges.

Consumer Abuse. Harm done to consumers by corporations.

Consumerist. You! A consumer who actively seeks compensation for flawed products or services.

Contingency Liability. What might go wrong for companies when they offer a deal, such as a surge in frequent fliers trying to redeem their frequent-flier points (God forbid).

Cost-Plus Contract. A no-bid contract granted by a small government agency to a large corporate entity for a massive project at a stupendous cost. The urgency of the project justifies elimination of competitive bids, vigorous oversight, and public discussion. See *Privatization*.

Covert Marketing. Activities designed to market images without the intended audience detecting that something is being marketed to them.

Critical Step. A procedure that must be done successfully to allow a process to continue and meet the specs required. Sometimes called a *choke point.*

CTA. *Call to Action.* Acronym or phrase to energize a consumer to act immediately to avoid losing a time-sensitive opportunity. Examples: *Limited Time Offer, Expires Soon, Available Only in this TV Ad,* and *While Supplies Last.* Here's another: Buy this book *while it's still in stock!* (Why do I like the ring of that one?) See also *Hot Buttons.*

Data Mining. Searching people's histories for marketing opportunities. For example, a search by a pharmaceutical corporation for physicians whose drug prescription histories "qualify" them to be marketing representatives.

Disemployment Rate. Rate at which employed consumers become unemployed due to outsourced job departure.

DIY. *Do It Yourself.* Examples: website customer service, voice-sensitive customer service, live chat customer service, and airport defibrillation devices. See DTA.

DM. *Dissatisfaction Management.* Isolation of the most determined dissatisfied consumers from all others.

DOD. *Defects on Delivery.* Problems known to corporations and discovered by consumers after product delivery.

DTA. *Drive Them Away.* Convince dissatisfied customers to give up and go away.

Due Diligence. Steps taken by accountants and bankers to avoid liability for not having been diligent enough.

Dynamically Priced Sports Tickets. Seats held back by

professional sports teams to be sold at a markup just before attractive games.

Early Cancellation Penalty. Variation: *Early Termination Penalty.* Imaginative penalties for consumers who, according to a corporation, fail to live up to the terms of a contract. Applies only to consumers, i.e., corporations are not obligated to pay "penalties" for failure to live up to their promises.

Expectation. Anticipation of consumers lured by promotional promises. Law of Expectation: The more imaginative the expectation, the greater the chance of disappointment. See *Benefits.*

Extended Warranty. An insurance policy offered to consumers to cover the costs of a defect that should have been fixed before the product was offered for sale.

FAQs. *Frequently Asked Questions.* Questions designed to change the subject or exhaust a consumer searching for answers.

Fees. Charges for unexpected costs sprung on unsuspecting consumers at unwelcome times. See *Hidden Fees, Obscured Fees,* and *Termination Fees.*

Food Miles. Distance between where food is grown and where it is sold. The greater the distance, the lesser the chance that "fresh" isn't so fresh.

Franchise. An arrangement whereby a national corporation has local presence without local liability. See *Plausible Deniability.*

Full Disclosure. 1. Traditional: Disclose what investors and regulators need to know to make fully informed decisions. 2. Corporate: Disclose as little as possible for as long as possible.

Golden Parachute. A clause in an executive agreement to enrich a key executive if he or she is forced to resign, no matter the cause.

Hidden Fees. Charges hidden from consumers until the opportunity arrives to collect them. See *Obscured Fees.*

Hold Music. Orchestral arrangements intended to soothe callers who expect a connection in less than twenty minutes. See also *Supermarket Music, Boutique Music,* and *Terminal Hold.*

Hot Buttons. Words and phrases proven to increase consumer response. Examples: *Free, Act Now, No Down Payment, Not for Sale to People Under 18, Organic, Fresh, Seedless,* and *Four-Hour Erection.*

Human Resources Department. A lagging indicator that a corporation is on the road to becoming too big to succeed.

KOLs. Pharmaceutical industry term for *key opinion leaders,* such as doctors, scientists, and others useful in the *covert marketing* of drugs for invented diseases.

Liquidification. Conversion of imagined assets into tangible money.

Mice Type. Used to "hide in plain sight" any words and phrases that might be grounds for future consumer complaints. Utilizes smallest type face allowed to tire a consumer's eyes early before meaningful words can be found.

Monetize. Conversion of free blogs and websites into sources for potentially tax-free income by site owners accepting ad links.

Money Laundering. Financial baptism of bad money reborn as good money. See *Stripping.*

Monopoly. Taboo term to be excluded from private memos or spoken in corporate buildings before 6 p.m. See *Near-Monopoly.*

MPT. *Multiple Prices Tactic.* Many prices simultaneously in play for the same item at the same time from supposedly competing businesses.

Near-Monopoly. Modern form of *monopoly.* Perfect *near-monopoly* leaves two corporations to divide markets as they see fit.

Obscured Fees. Charges camouflaged by small print in an odd location. See *Mice Type.*

OD. *Organizational Dysfunction.* Consequence of too many employees engaged in too many self-defeating activities that undermine organizational goals, such as making a profit or shipping a package.

Opening Night. Official night a theater production opens after having been open for several weeks of "previews." *Note:* A show may close before it opens. See *Previews.*

ORD. *Overwhelming Resistance Defense.* Deployment of deliberate delays and misdirections to break the will of dissatisfied customers.

Outs. Statements in sales pitches and promotions that anticipate consumer complaints after purchase of a product or service. See *Partial View.*

Partial View. A theater seat lacking full view of or sound from the stage, but sold a full price. *Note:* There is no current standard to define *partial* or requirement to disclose before selling a ticket.

Piercing the Corporate Veil. Attempt to penetrate barriers that cover up tax evasion, fraud, and book cooking.

Plausible Deniability. Political in origin, as in "I did not raise taxes; I raised fees" or "I did not have sex with that woman." Examples: Airlines on-time performance criteria and auto industry MPG projections.

Previews. 1. Legitimate theater: Four weeks before opening but during which consumers can purchase tickets for full price while improvements are made in the production. 2. Motion picture industry: 10–20 minute promotions of "coming attractions" with sound that can be heard within two blocks of the theater.

Privatization. Transfer of an industry from public to private ownership. The final stage is elimination of oversight and jobs.

Productification. Conversion of resources into a marketable consumer product. Resulting products may be eaten or worn by consumers or used to make another product by the company. May require chemical additives or new definitions of old words such as *cashmere.*

Productivity. 1. Eliminates need for details in reports of product and/or employee performance: *Our recent* productivity *study had promising results.* 2. Preceded by adjectives *greater* or *improved* in opening page of a report to stockholders after a difficult year: *I am pleased to report that greater* productivity *softened the impact of our losses.*

Provenance. 1. General: Information regarding the origins of valuable property, as for a work of art. 2. Gallerist: Information imaginatively treated to add value that previously did not exist.

QC. 1. *Quality Control.* Methods to maintain quality. 2. *Quality Communication.* Inclusion of the word *quality* in promotional materials and stockholders' reports.

Quality Fade. Slow elimination or replacement of procedures, components, and suppliers to increase profitability.

Retrospective. Repackaging a company's past products to retain or reinvigorate consumer demand.

Rigging. Navigation: Chains and ropes that manipulate sails to take advantage of the wind. Financial: Upward valuation of downward-headed securities.

Satisfaction. Consumer: Received benefits expected at cost anticipated. Corporate: Reached profit margin projected, and avoided excessive after-sale costs.

Securitization. A process by which bank and insurance executives package a few top-graded securities with many hopeless securities to form a whole seemingly worth more than its parts. Variation of *Bundling*.

Slamming. Calls made by fast-talking operators to get consumers to instantly and unknowingly switch phone service providers, as when AT&T was broken up and different carriers invented forms of alleged verbal agreements as "evidence" of agreement to switch.

Starburst. A profitable corporate part is worth even more if it is sold off. Example: CVS's Caremark, originally acquired to give consumers better mail order and website service, was considered a better asset if it could be sold.

Stripping. Removal of data after transfer of funds from one financial institution to another in a manner that conceals the transaction's origins in future transfers. *Stripping* originated with the Lloyds (of London) TSB Group to describe its process of concealing funds received from Iranian banks allegedly involved in financing Iranian nuclear weapon development. See *Money Laundering*.

Supermarket Music. 1. Selected by management to encourage shoppers to move swiftly through the aisles or be in tune with a storewide campaign to introduce a new food product. 2. Selected by employees to ease the burdens of doing their assigned work. See *Boutique Music* and *Hold Music*.

Synergy Fallacy. An imagined cost-saving from the merger of two large corporations.

Tax Shelter. 1. Traditional: Box number in Swiss bank account. Modern: Box numbers in Malta, Cyprus, Latvia, and several Caribbean islands.

Technodeterminism. Recent discovery that grants Internet entrepreneurs absolution from accountability for harm done to consumers by transfer of blame to technology as prime mover. See also *Best Practices*. For more, see Eli Pariser in *The Filter Bubble*.

Terminal Hold. Transfer of a caller to oblivion by automatic or human contrivance. Hold-time designed to make callers hang up, allowing corporation to designate the call as a*nswered-after-abandonment by caller.*

Transparency. Consumerist demand for disclosure of costs of executive retention, severance, and office furnishings.

Triage. Military: Battlefield division of wounded into hopeless, still fit for duty, and save-now/use-later. Management modification: Consumer complaints classified into easy-to-turn in minimal time, difficult but turnable, and send to a senior manager for resolution.

USIP. *Usual and Standard Industry Practice.* Corporate justification that whatever abuse happened is a long-standing industry tradition. Examples: 1. Interest rates on monthly credit cards. 2. Loan shark interest rates in the organized crime industry.

WACFAQ. *World Association for the Creation of Frequently Asked Questions.* Recently formed group for modernization of FAQs by basing FAQs on consumer reality rather than corporate fantasy.

WCD. *Weapons for Consumer Deterrence.* Tools and tactics that insulate a corporation from consumer complaints after purchase. See *FAQs.*

Windowing. Publishing practice of holding back the cheaper paperback edition until a hardcover book's sales decline.

WOPAS. *Window-of-Possible-Availability Service.* Systematic reduction of consumer appointments for service by requirement that consumers personally answer a test call to confirm their readiness for a technician. Failure to answer within three rings automatically cancels the visit without notice. *Helpful Consumer Note:* Leave this message on an answering device set for one ring. *Hello, technical support confirmation person. We are here but, due to the high volume of calls from other service people also scheduled for today, we are unable to answer your call. Your call is not as important as your scheduled visit. We are here. We really are. We are waiting. Just show up. Refreshments will be served upon arrival.*

FORMS FOR BATTLE PLANS

CORPORATE ABUSE RATING TOOL (CART)

Objectives

- Articulate how a corporate product or service abused you.
- Evaluate the effort you'll need to get compensation from the corporation.
- Recall and refine abuse(s).
- Get comp.

Think creatively about the wrongs that led to your dissatisfaction. The questions below may trigger memories you can use for ammunition. Have documentation ready. Inflate the "hurt" to negotiate. Be tough.

Deception and Manipulation: Were you misled by an ad? A salesperson? A brand name? Looking back, do you now see ways that a promotion or campaign might have played on your subconscious? (It's OK. You're human, and corporations are manipulative.) Do you see evidence of the manufacturer or distributor tinkering with the meanings of words? Was there a "stamp of approval" from an outside organization that seemed to certify that the product was safe, healthy, or would improve your life?

Rush to Market: If you were an early buyer of something, did you see signs of a less-than-perfect launch, perhaps early out-of-stock notices? Are telecoms dropping calls? Are you experiencing cable malfunction and cable company dysfunction? Are toll-free help lines telling you they're overloaded and directing you to the company's website?

Defect Toleration: Were there problems that suggest knowing neglect by a corportation or its supplier?

Quality Fade: Are unwelcome changes in familiar products accompanied by the word NEW! on the packaging?

Fulfillment Failure: Was delivery later than promised? Any damage to the contents? What is the evidence of damage? Need to take any pictures? Is the company willing to arrange for pickup and return? How much time will you need to make the return? How cooperative is the company? How much money do you need to spend to return a defective item?

Customer Disservice: Did Customer or Technical Service let you down or try to redirect you to a website? Were you unable to find your question in the list of FAQs? Does anyone who answers a toll-free call say, "May I put you on hold for a moment?" Did that representative try to transfer you to another expert or a different location? Did he or she waste of any of your time? Would he or she tell you his or her name or where he or she was located? Did he or she try to sell you anything?

Rate, Score, and Act

Use the CART Form (see next page) to rate the abuse(s) from 1 (bad) to 5 (terrible) and then the Compensation Evaluation Form (page 195) to determine the comp you are entitled to. Total the score and take appropriate action.

> 5–10: Consider minimal action, unless there are better targets.
>
> 11–20: Take action, spend moderate time on it.
>
> 21–30: Take strong action, spend maximum time on it.

Action

- Establish compensation target.
- Determine tactics.
- Attack at a time and place of your choosing.

CART FORM

Abusive Corporation: _____

Incident/Talking Points (summarize in 50 words or less):

Corporate Office Location(s): _____

Corporate Toll-Free Number: _____

E-mail: _____

Corporate Website: _____

[ ] SINGLE ABUSE [ ] ABUSE CLUSTER	DEGREE OF ABUSE Scale of 1 (bad) to 5 (terrible)
Deception & Manipulation	Score:
Rush To Market	Score:
Defect Toleration	Score:
Quality Fade	Score:
Fulfillment Failure	Score:
Customer Disservice	Score:

TOTAL SCORE: _____

COMPENSATION EVALUATION FORM

FORM OF COMPENSATION	NOTES & COMMENTS	VALUE TO YOU
Cash	The best for a consumer	
Partial Refund	Usually on a credit card	
Credit Against Future Purchase	Only good if consumer wants to continue the relationship	
Reduced or Cancelled Fees	S&H always a candidate	
Coupons	Free products or specific dollar value for buying specific products you use	
Courtesy Card	Only good if consumer wants to continue the relationship with the corporation	
Frequent Flier Points	Worth varies from one to five cents per point	
Replacement with Same Product	Insist on no charges and fast delivery	
Replacement with Better Product	Insist on no charges and fast delivery	
Added Services at No Added Charge	Free checking, phone numbers of special operators whom can be contacted, subscription extensions	

FURTHER READING AND USEFUL WEBSITES

Many authors in this list might be surprised—or alarmed—to learn of their inclusion in a handbook for consumerists. My criteria: Something of use to consumerists, said well, by an author who knows what he or she is talking about.

BOOKS

Ahamed, Liaquat. *Lords Of Finance: The Bankers Who Broke The World*. Penguin Group, 2009.

By accident (or perhaps by the forces of Intelligent Design) the author was working on this book about the roles of leading bankers in the causes of the Great Depression of 1929, a couple of years before the 2008 financial collapse. Change the dates and the players to see the identical propensity for delusional thinking that takes bankers off the cliff and us with them. The *Financial Times* (and, God help us, Goldman Sachs) called this a Business Book of the Year.

Glenny, Misha. *McMafia*. Borzoi Books, 2008.

As a writer for the *Economist* in 2007, Glenny added Organized Crime to the fourteen international industries listed in *The Economist 2007 Annual Review*. Glenny based his conclusion on evidence that later appeared in this book. He overcame the problem that since organized crime companies are not publicly held, they do not issue annual reports, thereby making their earnings and power harder to uncover without getting shot. It is amazing that Mr. Glenny has not "disappeared."

Ingrassia, Paul. *Crash Course: The American Automobile Industry's Road from Glory to Disaster*. Random House, 2010.
Ingrassia's background as Detroit Bureau Chief for the *Wall Street Journal* makes him well positioned to charge GM's management and union for their roles in demolishing a corporation once considered the best of the twentieth century. The lesson is that when management and labor are left to their own devices, what may be good for them is very bad for us.

Kay, John. *The Long and the Short of It*. The Erasmus Press, London, 2009.
An economist, Kay suggests readers are better off managing their own financial investments than wealth management professionals. A convincing contrarian, he argues that financial service corporations have their own reasons to buy and sell recommendations, which often ends in abused investors and no-lose results for the corporations.

Midler, Paul. *Poorly Made in China*. Wiley, 2009.
A narrative and analysis of why and how products undergo "quality fade" in China. Without directly saying so, Midler shows how American companies become compliant in and profit from quality fade. See also Midler's article "Dealing with China's 'Quality Fade,'" (www.forbes.com, July 26, 2007) where he first coined the term "quality fade."

Morgenson, Gretchen, and Joshua Rosner. *Reckless Endangerment: How Outsized Ambition, Greed, and Corruption Led to Economic Armageddon*. Times Books, 2011.
If any more evidence is needed of how much progress the financial services industry has made in capturing control of

American wealth—or that those in charge need adult supervision and regulation—this book will close the case.

Nestle, Marion. *What to Eat.* North Point Press, 2006.
In this excellent guide to intelligent nutritional choices, Nestle examines the steps involved in getting food to the supermarkets. She relates the business processes to profit-driven corporate claims about nutrition and our health.

Ogilvy, David. *Confessions of an Advertising Man.* Dell, 1963.
A phenomenally successful ad man and agency owner, Ogilvy helped cast the mold for the ad man stereotype portrayed in the TV series *Mad Men* and (more importantly) the nature of promotional ads that make promises that consumerists can use to make corps pay comp.

Packard, Vance. *Hidden Persuaders.* IG Publishing, 2007.
Originally published by Simon & Schuster in 1957, it was a runaway best seller that explained in plain English how the ad industry used legitimate motivational research to fashion ad campaigns aimed at our "hidden" desires.

Pariser, Eli. *The Filter Bubble: What the Internet Is Hiding from You.* Penguin Press, 2011.
An enlightening exposé on how hidden personalization technologies used by Google, Amazon, IBM, Apple, and others can tailor advertising on a person-by-person basis based on a person's seemingly private Internet activity.

Parkinson, Northcote C. *Parkinson's Law.* Ballantine Books, 1957; and upgraded into *Parkinson: The Law Complete,* Ballantine, 1980.

Parkinson's laws have passed into everyday usage and modification: A task takes as long as the amount of time scheduled for it. Expenditures rise to the amount budgeted. Parkinson speaks best for himself, "Work expands so as to fill the time available for its completion."

Petersen, Melody. *Our Daily Meds*. Picador, 2008.
A well-documented expose of how leading pharmaceutical corporations rig studies to come out favorably for their products in order to "help" patients deal with diseases in ways that do them little good and often a lot of harm. Petersen covered the industry for four years for the *New York Times*.

Petraeus, General David. *Counterinsurgency Field Manual*. University of Chicago Press, 2007.
Why is this book about fighting a war of interest to consumerists? Just read the foreword by Colonel Nagl and the introduction by Sarah Sewall to learn how decision-making models of corporations and armies are based on battles past rather than future, thus preparing you for your own war against corporate abuse.

Rost, Dr. Peter. *The Whistleblower*. Soft Skull Press, 2006.
The subtitle bills this as "Confessions of a Health-Care Hit Man" and while it is that, finding the confession requires sifting through accusations and allegations about how Dr. Rost was treated when Pfizer bought Pharmacia, his employer at the time. It is instructive (even if only half true) about the lengths to which large healthcare conglomerates go to cover up liability and avoid bad publicity for the problems their drugs may do.

Surowiecki, James. *The Wisdom of Crowds*. Random House, 2005.
A refreshing angle on how economics and industries operate.

He argues that experts are less reliable than the word implies, particularly when making predictions about future events based on past experiences. Surowiecki is a regular contributor to the *New Yorker*.

Truss, Lynn. *Talk to the Hand: The Utter Bloody Rudeness of the World Today, or Six Good Reasons to Stay Home and Bolt the Door*. Gotham Books, 2005.
Truss's complaint is our complaint: The unacceptable transfer of effort from corporations to consumers in matters of making and servicing products—and everything else.

Wilson, Bee, *Swindled*. Princeton University Press, 2008.
A carefully researched, well-written historical book about dangerously altered food, adulterated and flavored in Europe (especially England) and the United States. Bee examines of how legislators and regulators have cooperated with business interests and set the historical precedents for what we face with the food industry today.

Yellin, Emily, *Your Call Is (Not That) Important to Us*.
Free Press, New York, 2009.
This book is included to demonstrate the futility of trying to find "middle ground" with the enemy. In an attempt to tell the stories of both the corporations that provide toll-free numbers and the frustrated people who end up swearing at operators, Yellin becomes overly sympathetic with the folks who answer the calls and misses the root cause: defects, poor service, and loss of consumer time. It is a wonder more callers do not swear at operators.

ARTICLES

Darlin, Damon, "What the Naïve Consumers Don't Know,
    Can Help You," *New York Times*, July 22, 2006.
Two Harvard professors discuss the ways major hotel chains
and mail order companies camouflage their "shrouded fees"
that are not stated or stated unclearly.

Duhigg, Charles, "Aged, Frail and Denied Care by Their
    Insurers," *New York Times*, March 26, 2007.
An investigative report on how leading insurers erect bureaucratic
obstacles to deny payment to the elderly and infirm trying to
collect for long-term health care.

Hicks, Jonathan, "Sales Practices At Dell Draw New York Suit,"
    New York Times, May 17, 2007.
A report on New York's State Attorney General suit against Dell
Computers for alleged bait-and-switch tactics and "failing to
provide customers with adequate support and repair services."

Jack, Andrew, "A Sugared Pill," *Financial Times*, March 9, 2011.
An update on the "cozy financial relationship" that pharmas
have with physicians and university professors who are
compensated in a variety of ways to endorse, present, and
otherwise support prescription drugs.

Martin, Andrew, "Lean Crop of Dollars," *New York Times*,
    October 4, 2007.
Analysis of the $109 billion subsidies in 2006 split between
"Commodity Crops" and my favorite, "Specialty Crops," such
as seedless watermelons.

McCartney, Scott, "Why Airlines Keep Losing Your Luggage,"
   Wall Street Journal, January 16, 2007.
This discussion on the decreased caps on liability increasing
the amount of luggage lost by airlines exemplifies how large
corporations successfully lobby regulators for lower costs that
ultimately result in less customer care.

Mueller, Tom, "Slippery Business: The trade in adulterated
   olive oil," *New Yorker Magazine*, August 13, 2007.
A carefully researched report on the extent of corruption,
outright fraud, and corporate compliance in the growth,
distribution, and labeling of expensive "Italian" olive oil. The
compliance by Italian trade association, the slow-to-act
approach of the EU, and the corruption of Italian officialdom
are all explained by the profit margins from what can be
passed off as premium olive oil.

Neuman, William, "Hidden Ingredient: The Sweetener,"
   New York Times, February 25, 2010.
This story of how tomato vendors sold tainted tomatoes by
paying bribes to purchasing managers at Safeway, B&G Foods,
and Frito Lay gets at the corporate agriculture industry standards
and practices that lead to deception, certification illusion, and
defect toleration.

Richtel, Matt, "Cable's Costly Grip on America's TVs,"
   New York Times, May 24, 2008.
This report on the rise of cable subscriptions includes comments
that describe the rationale by cable companies for their "bundling"
tactics and the relative low usage of the components in those
bundles that consumers are forced to purchase.

Stross, Randall, "When Mobile Phones Aren't Truly Mobile," *New York Times*, Digital Domain article, July 22, 2007.
American telcoms limit the mobility of mobile phones by locking customers into services and devices provided only by the telcom phone provider. In other words, a telcom will try to stifle competition from other companies by programming their phones to only work with their service. They also create contractual language that threatens inflated "early termination" fees.

Tugend, Alina, "Far From Always Being Right, the Customer Is on Hold," *New York Times*, May 24, 2008.
Tugend's personal experiences with Customer Service as it has moved from live operators to automated exemplify much of the customer disservice talked about in this book.

Womack, James, "Why Toyota Won," *Wall Street Journal*, February 13, 2006.
This article summarizes why the American auto industry has come undone. One of the five points is "GM and Ford still treat customers as strangers engaged in one-time transactions."

WEBSITES

The Internet is in the Wild West stage of its development. Anyone can "publish" anything. There is no assurance that what you read is fact-checked or even fact-checkable. The background of the writer(s) may be intentionally hidden or obscured. Monetization influences what is said and not said. Ads may appear on the side or pop up later. They may be ongoing and out of sight in many ways for many reasons. They may be dictated by data mining. A site or blog may be a front for gathering information that a visitor innocently provides in order to use the site.

Vigilance is needed. Here are three cautionary tales that illustrate why.

Amazon wants to stay tax-free. As this book goes to press, an attempt by California to collect sales taxes from residents making purchases on the Internet is being opposed by Amazon (and other Internet behemoths) along with a threat to close their California operations. Amazon wants to receive the services and benefits of being in California—highways, water, cleaner air, high density of Internet technology experts—but doesn't want to be part of collecting sales taxes to support those benefits because doing so would impact its business plan. By selling products without collecting sales taxes, Amazon can offer products at lower prices than its competitors in brick-and-mortar stores that carry the same products but are required to collect sales taxes. In effect, the lack of sales tax acts as a back-door subsidy that allows Amazon pricing flexibility to undercut competition, and it contributes to the mushrooming deficits of many states.

"Helpful" blogs can be the work of crooks. Also as we go to press, a case in Federal Court awaits a ruling by a judge. It indirectly involves the blog www.PissedConsumer.com that is allegedly part of a scheme by its owner, Opinion Corp. The blog allows consumers to post a complaint about a corporation that sold them a product or service they aren't happy with. It caught my attention because it had what appeared to be a solid database of past offenses and offenders. However, when I tried to learn more about its corporate ownership and blog authorship, it did not disclose much about Opinion Corp.

An Internet search led to a public record in which Opinion Corp, whose revenues appear to be in the millions, is accused of "racketeering, conspiracy and extortion"[26] by Ascentive LLC, represented by the law firm Flaster Greenberg. It alleged that PissedConsumer first gathers consumer complaints and once enough complaints are "published" against a corporation, PC contacts the corporation and offers a way to remove the complaints as part of a "service," *Custom Reputation Management* (CRM). This type of scheme is consistent with what I've encountered in many "free" blogs and website. The lawsuit proposes that CRM is really in the business of extortion and should be subjected to the RICO laws (Racketeer Influenced and Corruption Act). An attorney from the firm, Alexis Arena, said, "Cases like this are just the start."

Consumer protection is off-limits in a globalized world. The Internet can erase consumer protection when borders are electronically crossed. How can a resident of Pennsylvania be protected from an outfit in Rumania or Tasmania or Nigeria that dreams up an Internet-driven scam designed to get credit card or personal checking account numbers? No state or federal agency has jurisdiction beyond its borders, so globalization gets around the old protections—and right now there is little we can do to stop this.

* * *

With a little diligence, you can find useful resources online by conducting searches with keywords such as *consumer, consumerist, blogs, bloggers,* and *customer* or *consumer service problems.* Often using a well-known corporation with a couple of these words can produce helpful results. But use caution: Not all websites and blogs that use these words are our allies. The proof is in their posts, their relationships, and their techniques.

Here are a few good ones that I have found:

Bucks is a blog by *New York Times* columnists who also appear in the print version of the *Times*. I recommend Ann Carrns who writes most of the posts and Ron Lieber who is best known for his weekly column *Your Money*. Both cover a wide range of carefully researched subjects of value to consumers. So far there is no sign that monetization is abusing consumer or reader trust, but the day might come when site access will not be free (presently, limits exist for non-subscribers of the NYT). **bucks.blogs.nytimes.com**

Consumer Watchdog is a new group of consumer websites that initially started with consumer problems of interest to residents of Connecticut: **ctwatchdog.com**. It has expanded to Florida **FlaWatchdog.com** and Massachusetts **MassWatchdog.com**. Additional states are likely to follow. Started by veteran reporter George Gombassy, the sites use a newspaper style format, making many stories easily accessible on a page. The sites employ professional journalists who blog on health, diet, travel, and finance issues, and they also post selected consumer complaints. The sites are monetized, but there appears to be no conflict of interest as a result.

The Consumerist blog, **consumerist.com**, "found itself" when it broke away from Gawker Media in 2009 and became part of Consumers Union, publisher of *Consumer Reports*. I like its hard-hitting approach—"Shoppers bite back" is its motto—and strict resistance to the temptations of monetizing or any appearance of a conflict of interest (other than carrying a low-key "promo" to encourage a subscription to *Consumer Reports*). It deals with many of the same troublesome industries that this book has explored, and TC Archives and Topics can be helpful in organizing a skirmish. There is a "tip line" (347-422-6695) for consumers hoping the blog will go after an abusive corporation.

My personal favorite is the **Consumerist Manifesto Blog**. Full Disclosure: I own it, write it, and will never monetize it in any way, shape, or form. I started it in 2010 and invite readers of this book to become followers of the blog. It deals almost exclusively with my experiences, but since I buy lots of things and apparently have been permanently condemned to weekly abuse by the corporations from whom I buy things, you may find it useful or at least entertaining. The subscriber list belongs exclusively to me and will never be rented, loaned, or otherwise used for any purpose other to amuse and instruct consumers. Trust me. But verify. **www.consumeristmanifesto.net**

RipOff Report, **www.ripoffreport.com**, was started by Ed Magedson in 1995, making him a pioneer in providing a useful resource for consumers abused by corporations. RR's Consumer Tips are helpful for consumers new to consumerism. Access to RR is free, and it also offers an arbitration step, which might make sense for an expensive abuse, for a $2000 filing fee. Use of an arbitrator can be tricky and consumers should understand the terms and conditions before using arbitration of any kind. The site is monetized but, insofar as I can determine, it does not influence RR's editorial policies.

Wisconsin Consumer Protection Blog started in May 2011. It is written by Ivan Hannibal, a lawyer who heads a firm that specializes in Wisconsin-based consumer rights issues. If the post from May 22, 2011, sets the tone and content for this blog, consumerists should sign up. So far Hannibal's output has been limited, but if his summary of how AT&T overcharges customers is the kind of approach that will be seen again, it will stiffen the resolve of consumerists running into abusive behemoths like AT&T. **www.consumerrightslawoffice.com**

BOOK CLUB ACTION

PERSONAL NOTE FROM THE AUTHOR

Spread the word, consumerist comrades! You are a *gatekeeper* and may even be—dare I write it out loud—a **KOL**.

A book club is the perfect venue to bring the *Consumerist Manifesto* to life. Over cookies and coffee, we can help members get something back when they've been wronged by a corporation.

Let us conspire together. This book will pay for itself. If you have specific targets in mind, you now have the tools to launch your attack. If you have a book club, you have the venue for a weekly debriefing of your combat missions. Beats chatting about Jane Austen, doesn't it?

GENERAL DISCUSSION QUESTIONS

If I were at the meeting, here are a few of the questions I would ask along with some answers to get things rolling.

What are your expectations when you buy a product or service? I expect perfection when I buy anything. I am a customer who holds corporations to promises (often as interpreted by me) they make about my satisfaction. I start with high expectations. Seems to me that if a corporation thinks I am smart enough to buy what it sells, I am by definition qualified to decide whether my expectations were met. In other words, did I get my full money's worth?

Why do corporations treat us the way they do? They are more concerned with managing our dissatisfaction than generating our satisfaction.

Do corporations intentionally mislead consumers?
I think they do. Not everybody agrees, especially corporate board members and children who have small change as evidence of the tooth fairy. Discuss the intentions of hyperbolic ads or numerical claims like the AT&T campaign that its cell service covered 97% of Americans.

When corporations mislead, does it help consumerists if the corporations are penalized?
No. If penalized, it's never enough to change anything. Let them keep cheating, lying, and stealing. The vigilant among us will keep collecting.

Is the author odd?
That depends on what *odd* merans. Is it "odd" to like things as they are? Or is it "odd" to not use the coupons they send me? I give them to strangers I run into in the supermarket. The fun is in getting them. Now that may be odd.

Is the author spiritually defective?
I urge readers to exaggerate and fabricate as needed to reach their compensation goals. Some may see this as inconsistent with the Old Testament, the Ten Commandments, the New Testament, or the Boy/Girl Scout Pledge. On the other hand I'm just doing unto them as they do unto me. If it is good enough for a corporation, it is good enough for me. Amen.

ACTION QUESTIONS FOR BATTLE-READY BOOK CLUBBERS

Has a corporation abused you lately?
Think about something that happened to you in the last six months that, according to this book, would qualify as a corporate

abuse. Were there cluster possibilities? Assign a dollar value to the cost of buying the product and your time needed to bring it to the attention of someone who cares.

Did this book give you a plan of action for a product or service that recently let you down?
Suggestions: Start with what went wrong. Keep it short—under two minutes. Then consider these three big questions: How will you implement your plan? How will you measure results? If your initial action is ignored or rebuffed, what is your contingency plan?

Is there an official you can contact?
Although they try to be insulated from consumer complaints, officers and top-level managers cannot completely hide their addresses. You are unlikely to reach them in person. A subordinate will do if they are smart enough to realize that you are not just unhappy, you are also smart enough to overcome the barriers the corporation placed in your way. That person may have authority to deal with your issue before it gets out of hand. If you're perceived as a threat to the bottom line, all the better.

Revisit: How will you measure results?
This is another way of asking, How do you value your time? Are you keeping track of the time you're spending to find assistance? If a corporation is making it hard to reach anyone or find an answer anywhere, it is not accidental. You may need to revisit and increase the comp needed to make things right.

Let's do a "first reaction test."
For each corporation I name, make a thumbs-up or a thumbs-down sign, based on your negative or positive first reaction:

AT&T. Comcast Xfinity. Warner. Apple. American Airlines. Continental Airlines. General Motors. Google. Hewlett-Packard. Microsoft. Toyota. United Health Care. Verizon. Whole Foods. Pick your own. What accounts for the number of negative or positive reactions?

If more consumers were to adopt the author's approach, what would happen?
Better consumer cash flow? More consumer laughter? The end of corporations as we know them? (Two out of three is OK.)

ROLE-PLAYING
Assume that you are the author of this book. You are interviewed on a radio talk show. How would you respond:

- You readily admit that you exaggerate and manipulate. Maybe even lie. Aren't you no better than the corporations you criticize?
- You expect perfection in an imperfect world. A lot of people might say to you, "Grow up!"
- Suppose I am not satisfied with your book because it did not meet my expectations. Will you give me my money back?

Questions for corporate CEOs. Assume that you are the CEO of a large corporation that just recalled a product. Your publicist advises you do a taped interview. How would you handle these questions:

- Pharmaceutical: Don't you spend more on marketing and promotion than on research? How does that benefit the consumer?
- Telecom: Since you own a telecommunications company, why does it take so long for a customer to get to a live

operator who speaks perfect English and knows the product or service being called about?

- Financial services industry: We hear a lot about the need for more transparency in your industry. What do consumers need to know that corporations do not want to reveal?
- Supermarket chain: You grow nothing that you sell. When was the last time you visited the farm of a major supplier of the food you sell me?
- Department store chain: Why do prices for some garments or cosmetics rise or fall in your store in tandem with competitors' stores? Isn't that price fixing? How much space in your stores is rented but made to look proprietary?
- Automaker: How do you monitor your authorized dealers and service centers? Have you ever de-authorized any of them for mistreatment of consumers?

Sometimes I have to remind myself that I am not making up
the stuff in this book and corporations really do treat consumers
this way. Like any author, I have taken some "liberties" here
and there to amuse you, but never with the compensation and
information intended to inform you. In other words, I haven't
imagined or exaggerated the episodes that I have written;
I have reported them. In doing so, I have an obligation to give
credit for other people's words when I am using them. Most
sources will appreciate the recognition. A few probably would
have preferred I not quote what they said. I apologize in advance
for any "lifts" that I should have recognized and unintentionally
left out.

Introduction: Guerilla Warfare for Consumerists
1 See Lt. Colonel John A. Nagl's introduction, *The United States
Army Marine Corps Counterinsurgency Field Manual*, page xviii
(University of Chicago Edition, 2007).

PART ONE: BE EVER VIGILANT FOR CORPORATE ABUSES
2 "There's No Business Like Corporate Business" owes its
inspiration to the famous lyrics and music of Irving Berlin,
"There's No Business Like Show Business" from the musical
comedy *Annie Get Your Gun*, 1946.

Chapter 1: Deception and Manipulation
3 See the 1964 *Surgeon General's Report on Smoking and Health*
available online from the National Library of Medicine.
4 For more, see Burkhard Bilger, "Swamp Things," *New Yorker*,
April 20, 2009.
5 Letter from Robert C. Keeney, Deputy Administrator, USDA
Fruit and Vegetable Programs, July 21, 2010.

6 Letter from David Shipman, June 10, 2009. He was an advisor to President Obama in the 2008 presidential campaign and later appointed to the USDA in a marketing role.

7 From the website of AYCO Farms, 2006.

8 From an e-mail from Matt Goldthwaite, Dulcinea Corporation, March 3, 2006.

9 For the USDA's definition of *Organic Farming* visit their National Agricultural Library site, Publications tab, scroll down to "Sustainable Agriculture: Definitions and Terms. 1999, updated 2007," and search on that page for "organic farming" or enter the following URL into your browser: http://www.nal. usda.gov/afsic/pubs/terms/srb9902terms.shtml#term23.

Chapter 2: Too Big to Succeed Meets the Rush to Market

10 See Bob Hagin's *Technical: Diesel Redux*, November 6, 1998, at: http://www.theautochannel.com/news/writers/bhagin/1998/ fs9845.html

Chapter 4: Outsourcing—The Road to Quality Fade

11 Written by David Witman, Nordstrom, May 28, 2010.

12 Written by Paula Pryor, Bloomingdale's Executive Office, March 18, 2010.

13 Laura Scholz, *How to Buy a Good Cashmere Sweater* at: http://www.ehow.com/how_2323623_buy-good-cashmere-sweater.html.

14 Written by Tim Dexter, buyer of housewares at Walmart, February 8, 2010.

Chapter 5: Fulfillment Failure

15 *New York Times* 2007 *Annual Report*, p 1.

Full disclosure: I am a *New York Times* shareholder.

Chapter 6: Customer Disservice

16 James Surowiecki, "Are You Being Served?" *New Yorker* September 6, 2010. Also see my letter describing service as even worse, published in the *New Yorker* on September 20, 2010.

17 Covad e-mail letter "Welcome AT&T Worldnet/DSL Customer" sent March 9, 2010.

PART TWO: FIGHTING BACK THE RIGHT WAY—GET THE CASH

Chapter 7: Know the Enemy's Mind and Tactics

18 Page 163: Woody Allen, "A Look At Organized Crime" reprinted in *The Insanity Defense* (Random House, 2007).

19 Reporting Organized Crime income is speculative. OC is privately held and its income statements are therefore hard to come by. Guy Dinmore of the *Financial Times*'s reported Sicilian Cosa Nostra's gross (based on well-founded estimates) in 2009 was at $182 billion. The FT's online archive is rich in stories of Mafia money.

20 Peter Kiefer, "Mafia crime is 7% of GDP in Italy, group reports" *New York Times*, October 22, 2007.

21 Guy Dinmore, "Mafia rushed to fresh profits through gap in the Berlin Wall," *Financial Times*, November 14, 2009.

22 Letter from Caludia Jeenan Hough, Director of Marketing, NYC Opera, May 6, 2003. It was followed by another letter (June 16, 2003) in which she changed her mind and gave us two tickets "to an opera of your choice" in the following season.

Epilogue: Where Things Are Headed

23 For a whole lot more on how and why this is happening, read *Terror and Consent: The Wars For The 21st Century* by

Phillip Bobbit (Albert Knopf, 2008). It is a startling read that is about more than war. "Chapter Two: The Market State" is required reading for any consumerist.

24 Joe Nocera, "The Travails of Ms. Warren", *New York Times*, July 23, 2011.

25 If you never read another article about Goldman Sachs and Lloyd Blankfein and John Paulson, or if you simply want to get angry all over again about how consumers have been ripped off by financial goons, try two short pieces: Christopher Caldwell, "Not malevolent but mediocre" in *Financial Times*, February 15, 2009, p 7; and Sebastian Mallaby, "Goldman's pieties insult our intelligence" *Financial Times*, January 13, 2011, p 9.

PART THREE: REFERENCES

Appendix C: Further Reading and Useful Websites
26 See press release from Flaster Greenberg, http://www. flastergreenberg.com/newsroom-news-Ascentive_LLC_Sues_PissedConsumer_com.html, with a link to a summary of the charges.

All art is collaborative. Whether you are a writer, composer, choreographer, designer, dancer, painter, sculptor, swindler, or whatever, artistic achievement rarely happens in a vacuum. I'd need several pages to thank everyone who helped me with this book, so space is reserved for a special few.

At the top is Matthew Blumberg, who knew I was working on this book and introduced me to Nathaniel Marunas at Sterling Publishing. As Matt put it, "you two deserve each other," a reference to our compatible (combustible?) attitudes about corporate abuse. No Matt, no Nathaniel; no Nathaniel, no book.

Looking for a title, I described my early ideas to Barbara Manfrey Vogelstein, who has a talent for cutting to what's important in a book. She said, "It's about consumer empowerment, right?" *Yeah,* I thought. *Empowerment—of course!* But my wife Patricia insisted my original title, *Never Give A Corporation An Even Break,* was my dumbest yet. Steve Longstreth, who can tell my consumerist stories and deliver the punch lines better than I, suggested *The Revenge of The Abused Consumer.* I liked it, but... Finally, Nathaniel came up with the just-right title, *The Consumerist Manifesto Handbook*—proof that authors need to listen as well as write.

The talents of three other collaborators can be seen everywhere in this book. The writing and editing talents of Ron Dicker and Sterling's own Katherine Furman helped me articulate and elevate my guerilla message. This book could not have happened without them. And in full display from the cover to the interior pages are the graphic talents of illustrator and designer Allison Meierding, who made the words and ideas "pop" in ways that remind me of Roy Lichtenstein.

Finally, where would I have been without all the bottom line-obsessed corporate CEOs, MBAs, and customer service managers, who are unintentional but invaluable collaborators of another sort when they churn out consumer abuses on an assembly-line basis that would surprise and awe even Henry Ford? Without what they do and how they think, this book could not have been written. Thank you all, every one.

THANK YOU
THANK YOU
THANK YOU
THANK YOU
THANK YOU
THANK YOU
THANK YOU
THANK YOU
THANK YOU
THANK YOU
THANK YOU